FLY-FISHING EQUIPMENT & SKILLS

THE HUNTING & FISHING LIBRARY®

By John van Vliet

Credits

JOHN VAN VLIET *is author of the best-selling book,* The Art of Fly Tying. *An avid trout angler, he has fly-fished throughout North America, England and New Zealand.*

JOHN RANDOLPH, *editor and publisher of* Fly Fisherman *magazine, is one of the most widely respected authorities on fly fishing. His writings have helped increase public awareness on issues of conservation and stewardship.*

DAVID TIESZEN *is an accomplished fly fisherman and expert flytier. A former guide on some of Alaska's premier streams, he has pursued a wide range of gamefish from Alaska to Florida.*

John van Vliet (left), John Randolph and David Tieszen on Armstrong's Spring Creek, Montana.

CY DECOSSE INCORPORATED

A **COWLES MAGAZINES COMPANY**

Chairman/CEO: Bruce Barnet
Chairman Emeritus: Cy DeCosse
President/COO: Nino Tarantino
Executive V. P./Editor-in-Chief: William B. Jones

FLY-FISHING EQUIPMENT & SKILLS

Author and Book Development Leader: John van Vliet
Executive Editor, Outdoors Group: Don Oster
Editor and Contributing Writer: Dick Sternberg
Technical and Editorial Consultant: John Randolph
Research and Technical Advisor: David L. Tieszen
Project Managers: Tracy Stanley, Denise Bornhausen
Senior Art Director: Bradley Springer
Contributing Art Directors: Dave Schelitzche, Stephanie Michaud
Copy Editor: Janice Cauley
Director of Photography: Mike Parker
Studio Manager: Marcia Chambers
Principal Photographers: Phil Aarestad, William Lindner
Staff Photographers: Mike Hehner, Mark Macemon
Photo Assistants: Mike Hehner, David L. Tieszen
Contributing Photographer: Lance Vicknair
V.P. Development, Planning and Production: Jim Bindas
Senior Production Manager: Gretchen Gundersen
Senior Desktop Publishing Specialist: Joe Fahey
Production Staff: Mike Schauer
Illustrator: Chad A. Peterson

Contributing Individuals and Agencies: Eugene Altwies; Tom Andersen – Andersen Sales; George Anderson – The Yellowstone Angler; John Bailey – Dan Bailey's Fly Shop; Berkley; Gary Borger; Bill Bornhausen; Burger Brothers – Fred Ardoff, John Edstrom, John Goplin, Dave Johnston; Cabela's; Cliff Lake Lodge – Mark & Sherrie Stokman; Philip Hanyok; Hobie Outback – Bill Horner; Bob Jacklin – Jacklin's Fly Shop; Capt. Jake Jordan; Lefty Kreh; LaCrosse Footwear; Mark Larson – D. B. Dunn, Partridge of Redditch; G. Loomis – Bruce Holt, Rori Homme, Steve Rajeff; Craig & Jackie Mathews – Blue Ribbon Flies; Jim Moynagh; O. Mustad & Son; Old Town Canoes – Great Northern Group: Roy Kraft, John Wright; The Orvis Company – Paul Ferson, Tim Joseph, Tom Rosenbauer; PAL – Dave Fuller; Peerless Reels – Robert Corsetti; Rodcraft – Dave & Chad Peterson; Sage Manufacturing Corporation – Marc Bale, Don Green, David T. Low, Jr.; St. Croix Rod Company – Rich Belanger, Linda Grassl, Jeff Schluter; Scott Fly Rod Company – Todd Field, Stephen D. Phinny; Simms; Capt. Danny Strub; 3M/Scientific Anglers – Jim Kenyon; Umpqua Feather Merchants; Bob White; Joan Whitlock

Printed on American paper by: R. R. Donnelley & Sons Co. (0296)

ISBN 0-86573-056-3

CONTENTS

INTRODUCTION · · · · · · · · · · 4

FLY-FISHING EQUIPMENT · · · · · · · · 6

FLY RODS · · · · · · · · · · · · · · 8
REELS · · · · · · · · · · · · · · 15
FLY LINES · · · · · · · · · · · · · · 18
  Backing · · · · · · · · · · · · · · 23
FLY LEADERS & TIPPETS · · · · · 25
  Tying your own leaders · · · · · · · · 28
CLOTHING · · · · · · · · · · · · · · 30
ACCESSORIES · · · · · · · · · · · 36
WADING GEAR · · · · · · · · · · 45
TUBES & BOATS · · · · · · · · · · 50
FLIES · · · · · · · · · · · · · · 56
  Dry flies · · · · · · · · · · · · · · 58
  Nymphs · · · · · · · · · · · · · · 60
  Wet flies · · · · · · · · · · · · · · 62
  Streamers · · · · · · · · · · · · · · 64
  Terrestrials · · · · · · · · · · · · · · 66
  Bugs · · · · · · · · · · · · · · 68
  Specialty flies · · · · · · · · · · · 70
  Saltwater flies · · · · · · · · · · 72

MATCHING THE
TACKLE TO THE FISH · · · · · · · · 75
  Equipment for trout · · · · · · · · · · 76
  Equipment for steelhead &
    Pacific salmon · · · · · · · · · · 80
  Equipment for Atlantic salmon · · · · 81
  Equipment for sunfish · · · · · · · · 82
  Equipment for crappies · · · · · · · · 83
  Equipment for smallmouth bass · · · · · · 84
  Equipment for largemouth bass · · · · · · 86
  Equipment for pike & muskies · · · · · · 88
  Equipment for bonefish · · · · · · · · 90
  Equipment for tarpon · · · · · · · · 91
  Equipment for redfish · · · · · · · · 92
  Equipment for striped bass · · · · · · · · 93

FLY-FISHING SKILLS · · · · · · · · 95

FLY-FISHING KNOTS · · · · · · · · 97
  Attaching fly to tippet · · · · · · · · 98
  Joining monofilament · · · · · · · · 100
  Making a loop in a leader · · · · · · · · 102
  Joining fly line to backing
    or leader · · · · · · · · · · · · · · 104
  Making a loop in your fly line · · · · · · 106
  Joining loops · · · · · · · · · · · 107
  Making double-line connections · · · · 108
  Attaching shock tippet to leader · · · · · 110
  Attaching fly to shock tippet · · · · · 111
FLY CASTING · · · · · · · · · · · 112
  Getting started · · · · · · · · · · · 114
  Tips for practicing fly casting · · · · · · 115
  Elements of a casting stroke · · · · · · 116

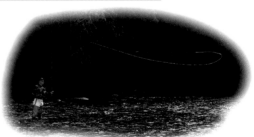

  Casting plane · · · · · · · · · · · 118
  Overhead cast · · · · · · · · · · · 120
  False cast · · · · · · · · · · · · · · 122
  Distance cast · · · · · · · · · · · 126
  Roll cast · · · · · · · · · · · · · · 130
  Mending line · · · · · · · · · · · 132
  Retrieving line · · · · · · · · · · · 136

GLOSSARY · · · · · · · · · · · 138
INDEX · · · · · · · · · · · · · · 140

Introduction

Before you can land a fish, or even cast a fly, you should become familiar with the tools of the sport and develop the skills to use them effectively.

The first section, "Fly-Fishing Equipment," will help you select the right gear for the type of fishing you plan to do. Then, once you've selected a balanced rod, reel and line, and assembled the necessary clothing and accessories, we'll help you choose the right flies for the fish you're after.

The second section, "Fly-Fishing Skills," begins by teaching you the basic knots for making leaders, connecting them to the fly line and tying on flies.

Then, you'll learn the most important skill in fly fishing: casting. We'll explain the function of every important cast and, using step-by-step color photography, show you exactly how to make it.

Too many beginning fly anglers buy expensive gear and every gadget available, but soon become discouraged and give up because they aren't catching fish. The problem is, they bought the wrong equipment and never learned to use it properly. This book will lay the proper groundwork for a sport that could well become a lifetime passion.

FLY-FISHING
EQUIPMENT

Fly Rods

The fly rod is the single most important tool in fly fishing. It is used to cast the fly line, which, in turn, delivers the leader and the fly. The rod is also important in controlling the line on or in the water, and in playing a fish once it is hooked.

Fly rods come in a wide range of styles and prices depending on the type of fishing you plan to do, and your budget. When choosing a fly rod, consider material, action, length and weight designation.

MATERIAL. What a rod is made of determines its weight, cost, and how it performs on the water.

The earliest fly rods were made from woods such as ash, hickory, willow and greenheart, a South American hardwood. These long, heavy rods were used to place, rather than cast, a fly.

8

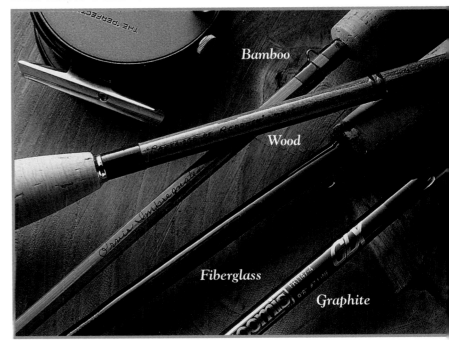

Bamboo

Wood

Fiberglass

Graphite

By the 1850s, a number of American rodbuilders were experimenting with slender strips of split bamboo glued together to form a single blank (center right). Bamboo, or *split-cane*, rods were remarkably strong, yet flexible. Consequently, they could be made lighter for their length than earlier wood rods.

But bamboo rods were expensive and required regular maintenance, such as revarnishing, and careful storage to prevent warping. To solve these problems, a number of rodbuilders began to impregnate the bamboo with synthetic resins.

Fiberglass rods were introduced in the late 1940s, and quickly eclipsed bamboo in popularity. They were cheaper and more durable, and could be mass produced. These early fiberglass rods were made from solid blanks, so they lacked rigidity,

BAMBOO *rod building has changed little over the last 150 years. Blanks are still built by hand from slender strips of split cane glued together to form a hexagonal blank (inset).*

GRAPHITE *rods are made from sheets of carbon-fiber material wrapped around a tapered steel form, called a mandrel.*

PARTS OF A FLY ROD

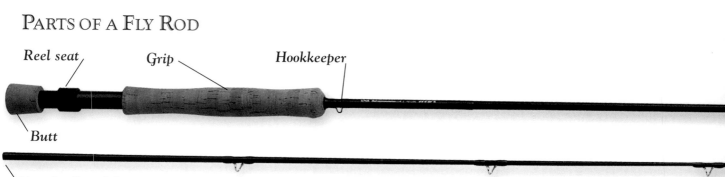

Reel seat   Grip   Hookkeeper

Butt

Ferrule (female)

resulting in unpredictable casting dynamics. By the early 1950s, however, rodbuilders were wrapping fiberglass cloth around a tapered steel form, or *mandrel*, to produce a hollow blank. This method greatly increased rigidity while reducing the overall weight of the finished fly rod.

In the 1960s, aerospace engineers developed graphite, a carbon-fiber material which, like fiberglass, was available as a cloth. But graphite is much stronger for its weight than fiberglass, giving it a higher stiffness-to-weight ratio, or *modulus*. As a result, graphite rods are lighter and thinner than bamboo or glass and produce higher line speeds for greater casting distance.

Graphite eventually replaced glass, and by the early 1980s, few fiberglass rods were being produced. Today, over 95 percent of all fly rods are graphite. But some manufacturers still add fiberglass to their graphite rods for durability and a handful continue to build high-quality, all-glass rods. Bamboo rods are still made in limited numbers and remain the finest examples of the rodmaker's craft.

ACTION. There is no common definition of fly-rod action, and most manufacturers do not even designate the action of their rods. But action is important and is determined by two different characteristics. The first is how and where the rod bends under a load (chart, opposite page), as it does when casting a line. The second is how quickly it recovers from a bend, or *dampens*. Both of these characteristics are determined by what the rod is made of, its modulus and its *taper*, or the way in which the rod narrows from butt to tip.

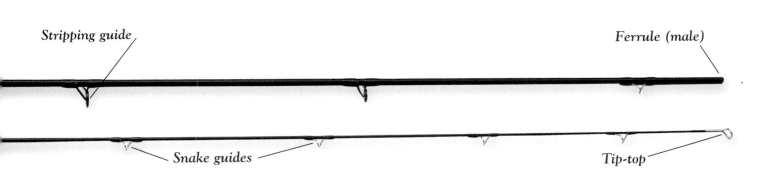

UNDERSTANDING FLY-ROD ACTION

A rod with a fast recovery rate is almost always preferable to one that recovers slowly. But recovery rates vary between individual rods and rods from different manufacturers, and there is no standard method of measurement.

LENGTH. Most fly rods fall into the 7½- to 9-foot range. Rods shorter than 7½ are popular with light-line or small-creek enthusiasts, while rods over 9 feet are used in special situations, such as float-tube fishing.

WEIGHT. Not to be confused with how much a rod weighs, the weight designation of a fly rod describes the size fly line the rod is designed to cast most effectively. In other words, a 4-weight rod is designed to cast a 4-weight line. Fly rods range in weight from 1 to 15, but the vast majority fall in the 3- to 12-weight range.

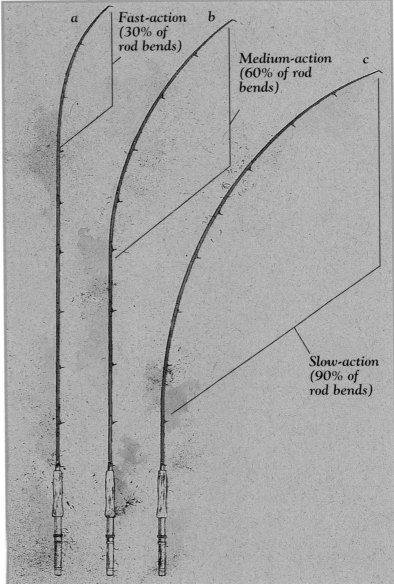

a
Fast-action
(30% of
rod bends)

b

Medium-action
(60% of rod
bends)

c

Slow-action
(90% of
rod bends)

A ROD that bends mainly near the tip during a cast is described as (a) fast action; one that bends into the midsection, (b) medium action; and one that bends into the butt section, (c) slow action. Fast-dampening rods are also said to have a fast action; slow-dampening, slow action.

11

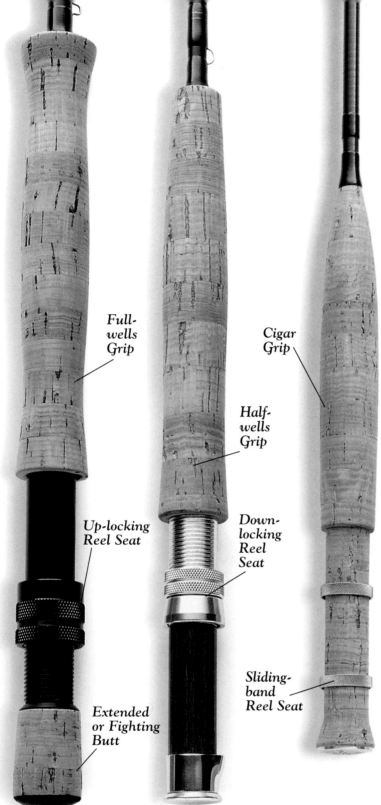

Full-wells Grip

Cigar Grip

Half-wells Grip

Up-locking Reel Seat

Down-locking Reel Seat

Sliding-band Reel Seat

Extended or Fighting Butt

POPULAR
GRIP STYLES
& REEL SEATS

GRIP STYLE. How a rod feels in your hand depends in part on the design of the grip. One that is too fat or too thin can make the whole rod feel awkward. There are as many grip styles as there are rodmakers; however, a few styles have become standard and are offered on most production rods. The most popular styles are the cigar, half-wells and full-wells (left).

The cigar grip is often used on lighter rods, for a more delicate feel; heavier rods generally have a full-wells grip, which is flared at both ends. The half-wells is flared at only one end, and used on intermediate-weight rods. A front flare provides extra leverage for your thumb; a rear flare allows room for the reel foot on uplocking reel seats (left). Select a grip that fits your hand and feels comfortable when casting.

REEL SEAT. Some light rods have sliding-band reel seats, with lightweight rings or bands to hold the foot of the reel. Medium and heavy rods usually have up-locking seats, which are more secure but require a thicker grip, because one foot of the reel slides under the grip. Down-locking seats are losing popularity, mainly because the reel is at the very end of the rod, making it difficult to place the butt against your body for extra fighting leverage.

12

MATCHING ROD AND LINE WEIGHT TO FLY SIZE

Rod/Line Weight	Fly Size Range	Rod/Line Weight	Fly Size Range
3	28 – 12	8	12 – 1/0
4	26 – 10	9	10 – 2/0
5	24 – 8	10	8 – 3/0
6	20 – 6	11	6 – 4/0
7	16 – 4	12	4 – 6/0

CONSIDER size of the flies you'll be using when choosing a fly rod. As a rule, the heavier your rod and line weight, the larger the fly you can comfortably and effectively cast.

ROD-CARE TIPS

ASSEMBLE fly rod by inserting butt section into top section with guides 90° out of alignment (right). Twist sections gently, while aligning guides, until tight (far right). If you push the sections together straight, it will wear a groove that can cause the rod sections to accidentally come apart.

To take rod apart, simply twist sections 90° while pulling.

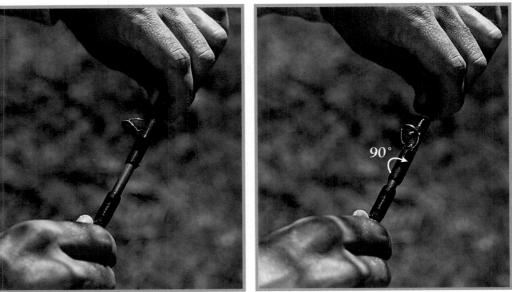

STORE your rod in a secure rod tube. Popular styles include: (a) aluminum with screw-on cap; (b) plastic; (c) cordura with PVC interior tube; (d) multirod; and (e) rod-and-reel style, for packing your fly rod with reel attached.

Reels

Some experts will tell you that a reel is simply a place to store line; but that's a little like saying a car's brake pedal is just a place to rest your foot. Today's reels perform a variety of functions and are far more sophisticated than they appear. Here are some considerations in fly-reel selection:

DRAG. A good, adjustable drag slows a running fish and prevents spool overrun. The larger the fish, the more important the drag becomes.

The most simple and common type of drag is the ratchet-and-pawl. An adjustable spring keeps the pawl pressed against the ratchet, making an audible click.

Disc-style drags perform like the disc brakes on a car, using the smooth friction of one large surface against another. They are a better choice for powerful fish such as steelhead and bonefish.

PARTS OF A REEL

FRAME

RATCHET-and-PAWL REEL

Pillar

Pawl, *presses against ratchet on spool to provide drag*

Drag adjustment *(knob on opposite side)*

Foot

SPOOL

Ratchet

Clicker

Disc drag surface

Spool release, *for removing spool*

Counterbalance, *to prevent spool wobble*

FRAME

Drag adjustment *(knob on opposite side)*

Handle

DISC-DRAG REEL

SPOOL

System 2

45L

Many reels have an exposed spool rim, which allows you to apply additional drag tension by pressing your open hand against the rim, a technique called *palming*.

MATERIAL. Fly reels are made from a variety of materials, including aluminum and graphite. Aluminum reels are the most common and come in all price ranges. Reels machined from a single block of aluminum alloy, called *bar stock*, can cost up to ten times as much as those stamped from sheet alloy. Aluminum reels intended for saltwater use are anodized for additional corrosion resistance.

Graphite reels are lightweight and offer a low-cost alternative to metal, but they are not as durable and their parts do not fit as precisely.

ACTION. A reel's action describes the rate at which it retrieves line. On a *single-action* reel, the most common type, the spool turns once for each turn of the handle, for a 1:1 retrieve ratio. Single-actions are light, durable and have few moving parts to fail. A *multiplying* reel has additional gearing that causes the spool to turn more than once for each

REEL MATERIALS include: (a) machined aluminum alloy; (b) stamped aluminum alloy; (c) anodized aluminum; and (d) graphite.

REEL ACTIONS include: (a) single-action, with 1:1 retrieve ratio, and (b) multiplier action, with 1.5:1 to 3:1 ratio.

REEL DRIVES include: (c) direct-drive, with handle that turns in both directions; and (d) anti-reverse drive, with handle that turns in only one direction.

SPARE SPOOLS are available for most reels. They allow you to switch fly lines quickly without changing reels. Use a line tender (arrow) to keep spool from unrolling. Mark line size and style on tender for easy identification.

turn of the handle, usually from 1.5 to 3 times, for a retrieve ratio of 1.5:1 to 3:1. Multiplying reels are frequently used for large fresh- and saltwater species and in situations where you need to take up line in a hurry.

DRIVE. Most reels are direct-drive, meaning that the handle rotates with the spool in either direction. But if a fish makes a fast run, the spinning handle can take the skin off your knuckles. Anti-reverse reels employ a clutch mechanism, which keeps the handle from spinning backward when a fish takes out line.

SIZE AND CAPACITY. The reel you choose should be designed to hold the size fly line you've selected with ample capacity for backing material (p. 23). The larger the fish you're after, the greater the capacity you'll need.

REEL-CARE TIPS

LUBRICATE reel periodically to keep it operating smoothly. Choose a lubricant designed for reels.

WASH a reel used in saltwater with fresh water and soap to prevent corrosion. Dry reel thoroughly before storing.

17

Fly Lines

The fly line distinguishes fly fishing from all other forms of fishing and makes it possible to cast an essentially weightless fly. The weight of the line bends, or *loads*, the rod, propelling the line, leader and fly.

Fly lines, which are typically 80 to 105 feet long, come in many weights, tapers and colors. Some are designed to float; others to sink at varying rates and to different depths. Still others are a combination of floating and sinking line segments. Your choice of line depends primarily on the size of your fly, the distance you want to cast it and the depth at which you want to present it. When choosing a fly line, consider:

STANDARD LINE WEIGHTS *(first 30 feet)*

Line Size	Weight	Line Size	Weight
#1	60 grains	#7	185 grains
#2	80 grains	#8	210 grains
#3	100 grains	#9	240 grains
#4	120 grains	#10	280 grains
#5	140 grains	#11	330 grains
#6	160 grains	#12	380 grains

LINE WEIGHT is measured in grains, and determines what size fly you can comfortably cast.

PARTS OF A FLY LINE *(weight-forward shown)*

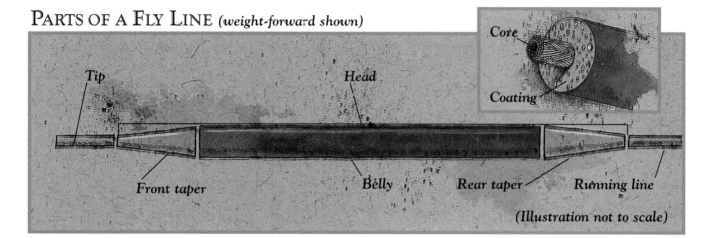

Tip • Head • Core • Coating • Front taper • Belly • Rear taper • Running line

(Illustration not to scale)

WEIGHT. Besides determining what size fly you can cast (p. 13), line weight also affects the distance of your cast and the delicacy of your presentation. For best casting performance, be sure your line is matched to your rod.

Lines range in weight from size 1 (the lightest) to size 12. You can buy special-purpose lines as heavy as size 15. Line-weight designation is based on the weight (measured in grains) of the first 30 feet of the fly line (chart, above).

Lightweight lines (sizes 1 to 4) are best for delicate presentations of tiny flies at short distances.

LINE WEIGHT is designated with a 3-part code on packaging to help you identify what type of line it is. A line marked DT-5-F, for example, is a double-taper, 5-weight, floating line. WF-8-S indicates a weight-forward, 8-weight, sinking line.

Mediumweight lines (sizes 5 to 7) cast well in most fishing situations and will handle a wide range of fly sizes.

Heavyweight lines (sizes 8 and above) are suited for casting large flies to big fish in fresh- or saltwater. They are recommended for long-distance casting or punching a fly into the wind.

TAPER. Variation in thickness of the line's coating along its length determine its taper, which dictates how it performs in the air and on the water. Following are the most common tapers:

Double-taper (DT) lines have a long belly section tapering to identical front and rear sections. Double-tapers are popular for light-line trout fishing where a delicate presentation is required. They cast well at short to medium distances and are ideal for roll casting (p. 130). Because both ends are identical, double-taper lines can be reversed when one end wears out, extending line life.

Weight-forward (WF) lines are designed with most of the weight in the first 30 feet, tapering quickly to a long, thin section called *running line*. Weight-forwards cast farther than double-tapers, are better for casting in the wind and are a good choice for beginners. But they do not roll-cast as well as double-tapers.

Some manufacturers offer special-purpose weight-forward lines. On a bass-bug taper, for instance, the weight is concentrated in a shorter head that is ideal for propelling large, wind-resistant flies. Saltwater tapers also have a compact head, along with a stiff core and a plastic coating designed to prevent the line-sag and stickiness problems that can reduce hot-weather casting performance in ordinary lines.

Shooting tapers (ST) have a short, compact head that is attached to a separate mono-filament or coated-Dacron running line. The head easily pulls the thin running line through the guides, enabling you to cast very long distances – over 100 feet. But the head lacks delicacy

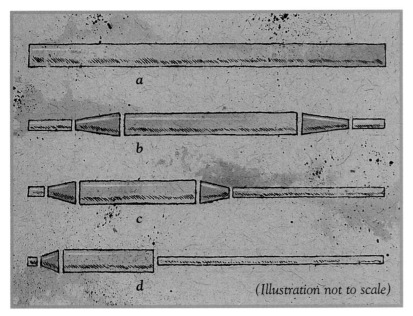

LINE TAPERS include: (a) level line, (b) double-taper line, (c) weight-forward line and (d) shooting taper, or shooting head, with separate running line.

and accuracy, and the running line tends to tangle easily. A stripping basket (p. 42) helps you control the running line.

Level lines (L) have a consistent diameter along their entire length. Although inexpensive, they are difficult to cast and rarely used.

BUOYANCY. Modern fly lines are carefully designed to float high or sink at a predictable rate. The right buoyancy depends on the type of fly you are using and how deep the fish are feeding.

Floating lines (F), the most popular type, have a coating impregnated with tiny air bubbles. Ideal for presenting dry flies, they are easy to cast and mend (p. 132), and won't pull the fly below the surface. They allow you to pick up and recast a fly quickly and easily.

Floating lines can be used for fishing subsurface flies by adding weight to the leader or fly, but in situations where the line prevents your fly from getting deep enough, a sinking line may be a better choice.

Sinking lines (S) vary in density, depending on the amount of lead or tungsten particles in the coating. Some lines are only a little denser than water, causing them to sink slowly.

TYPES OF SINKING LINES

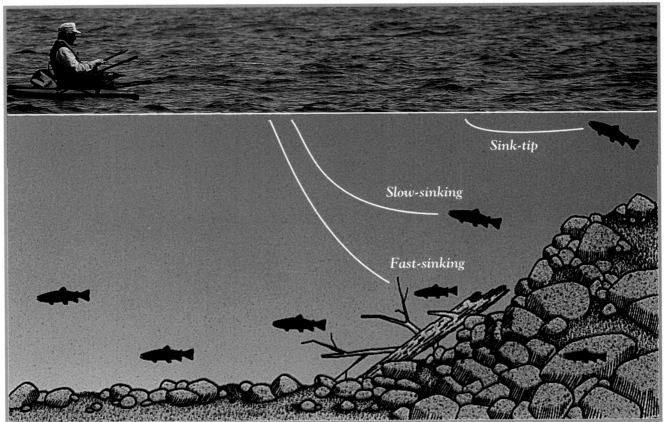

Others are denser and sink quickly, allowing you to fish at depths of 25 feet or more. With a sinking line, the entire length sinks, so the line can be difficult to control in the air and in the water, and you must retrieve most of the line before you can cast again.

Sink-tip, or *floating/sinking lines* (F/S), combine a long floating belly with a 5- to 25-foot sinking tip. The floating portion lets you control the line on the surface, while the sinking tip gets your fly down at varying rates, depending on line density. Sink-tip lines are easier to cast than full-sinking lines, but won't get as deep.

COLOR. Fly-line color is a matter of personal preference. Light-colored or fluorescent lines are a good choice for beginners, because they're easy to see on the water and in the air. Some anglers believe these colors spook the fish, but, in most cases, fish do not see the line because of the leader. Sinking lines come in darker browns and greens, making them less visible under water. The sinking portion of a sink-tip line is also dark, but the floating part is light-colored, to help you detect strikes.

LINE-CARE TIPS

CLEAN *fly line with mild soap and water to remove dirt. Do not use abrasives, which can damage line coating.*

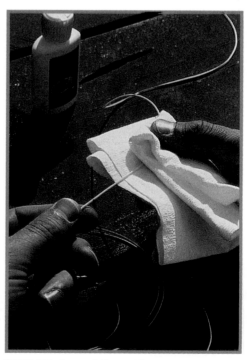

TREAT *cleaned line with a protectant to maintain plastic coating and help line shoot smoothly through guides.*

Backing

Without backing, a big fish could easily run out your entire fly line. Backing gives you the extra line you need to control the fish and connects your fly line to your reel. It also fills up the spool so you can reel in line more quickly.

The most common backing material is braided Dacron in 20- to 30-pound test. The average reel holds up to 150 yards of backing; big-game and saltwater reels, 250 yards or more.

HOW TO ADD BACKING

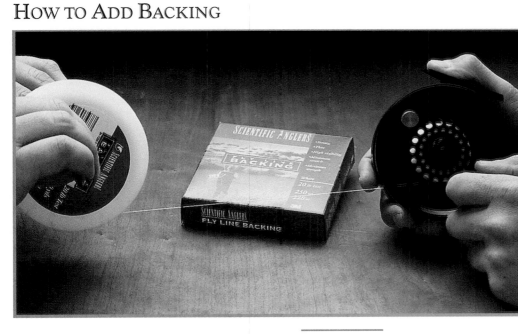

SECURE backing to reel with an arbor knot (p. 97), then wind on desired amount of backing directly from the spool, keeping tension on the backing so it winds on tightly. The amount of backing needed depends on its diameter, the size of the reel and the weight and type of fly line. Check the instructions that come with your reel for specific backing recommendations.

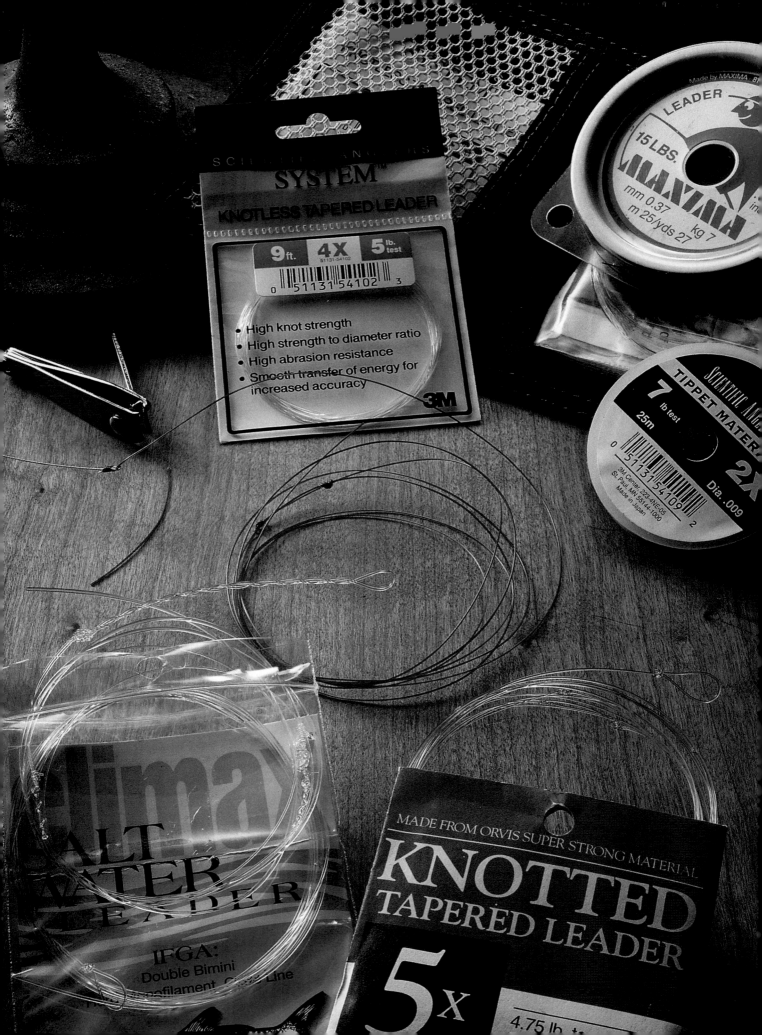

Fly Leaders & Tippets

The leader creates a nearly invisible connection between the heavy fly line and the fly. It also transfers the energy of the cast smoothly and efficiently, and helps give the fly a lifelike action on or in the water. These issues are important in leader selection:

MATERIAL. Until the 1950s, fly leaders were made from silkworm gut, which was strong and had low visibility, but became stiff and brittle when dry. Gut leaders required overnight soaking to make them supple enough for fishing.

Modern leaders come in a variety of man-made materials, which require far less care. They are available in a wide range of diameters, strengths, colors and hardnesses.

Nylon monofilament, by far the most popular leader material, is inexpensive, durable and nearly invisible, with excellent knot strength. But monofilament breaks down quickly in sunlight and will absorb water, causing it to weaken.

Braided nylon, though not as popular as it once was, cushions the shock of a hook set and turns over smoothly. But braided nylon is more visible than mono and, like mono, it absorbs water.

Polyvinylidene fluoride (PVDF) leader material, commonly called "fluorocarbon," is even less visible in water than nylon, because its refractive properties, or the way it bends light rays, more closely match the properties of water. It has 50 percent more abrasion resistance than nylon, but 50 percent less stretch, requiring a more gentle hook set to prevent break-offs with light tippets. PVDF is not affected by sunlight, and will not absorb water. However, it costs more and has poorer knot strength than mono.

TAPER. Most leaders taper from a relatively thick butt section to a fine tippet. As a result, the leader turns over easily and presents only the narrow-diameter tippet to the fish.

There are two types of tapered leaders: *knotted* and *knotless*. A knotted, or *compound*, leader is made up of several sections of different-diameter line, tied end to end. You can buy knotted leaders pretied, or tie your own to suit your type of fishing. There are countless formulas for tying leaders; see pages 28 and 29 for a few of the more common ones.

Knotless leaders taper gradually and may be a better choice for beginners or those unsure of their knots. They work well for fishing in vegetation, because there are no knots to catch weeds. They turn over well and are simple to use, but you may need to add tippet material when numerous fly changes shorten your leader.

LENGTH. The length of your leader depends on the type of fly and line you are using. When fishing dry flies, always use the longest leader you can comfortably cast, usually 7½ to 12 feet. For subsurface flies and sinking lines, use leaders shorter than 9 feet.

TIPPET DIAMETER. A tippet's diameter is measured using a system developed in the days of silkworm gut leaders. The gut was drawn through a series of decreasing-size holes in metal plates, reducing its diameter and producing a roughly uniform line. Each draw earned it another X. A 1X was the thickest; a 4X, the finest. Even today, a tippet's X-rating indicates its diameter, not its breaking strength; the same X-rating may have different strengths depending on the manufacturer (chart, opposite). Tippet material now comes as fine as 8X.

PARTS OF A LEADER

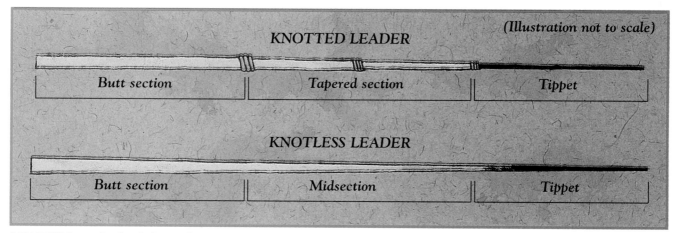

LEADERS *can be divided into three sections. The butt section makes up about 35-45 percent of the length; the midsection (tapered section in knotted leader), 40-55 percent; and the tippet section, 10-25 percent.*

TIPPET DIAMETER AND FLY SIZE

X-rating	Diameter	Breaking-strength Range*	Fly Size Range
8X	.003"	1.0 - 1.8 lbs.	28 - 20
7X	.004"	1.1 - 2.5	26 - 18
6X	.005"	1.4 - 3.5	22 - 14
5X	.006"	2.4 - 4.8	18 - 10
4X	.007"	3.1 - 6.0	16 - 8
3X	.008"	3.8 - 8.5	14 - 6
2X	.009"	4.5 - 11.5	10 - 4
1X	.010"	5.5 - 13.5	6 - 1/0
0X	.011"	6.5 - 15.5	2 - 3/0

Chart based on actual breaking strengths of popular brands of tippet materials. Breaking strength of a given X-rating varies greatly among manufacturers.

LEADER-CARE TIPS

LEADER WALLETS protect leaders and tippet material from sunlight. You may want to label the individual sleeves for easy identification of leader type and diameter.

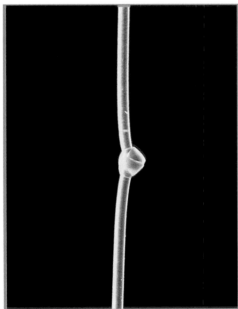

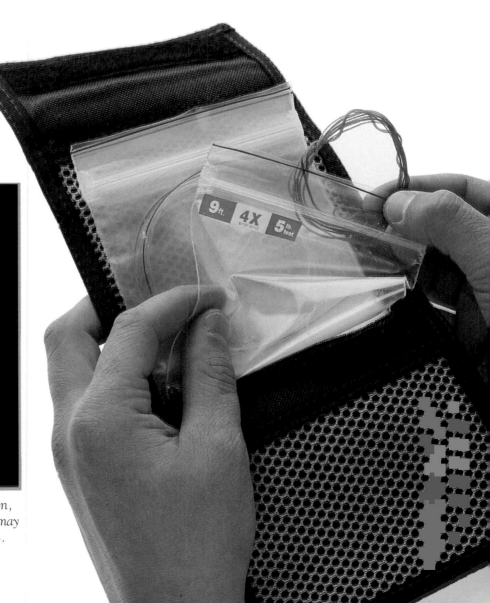

REPLACE your leader, or tippet section, if it develops a wind knot. These knots may reduce line strength by as much as 50%.

Tying Your Own Leaders

Most fly fishermen spend hundreds of dollars on a rod, reel and line, but give little thought to their leader. Yet no matter how good your rod and line are, a poorly designed leader won't turn over properly, and as a result will not deliver the fly accurately or delicately.

One solution is to build your own leaders. A well-designed leader has a stiff butt section and tapered midsection to turn over smoothly and carry the energy of the cast from the fly line through the leader; and a fine, soft-nylon tippet section that won't restrict the movement of the fly. By varying the length and stiffness of each of these sections, you can fine-tune your leader to suit your own casting style. If your tippet falls in a pile at the end of your cast, for example, try shortening it.

Leaders for saltwater and toothy freshwater species often include a wire or heavy mono shock tippet. Heavy saltwater leaders generally have tippets tied in with Bimini twists (p. 108) for maximum strength.

POPULAR LEADER FORMULAS *(Illustrations not to scale)*

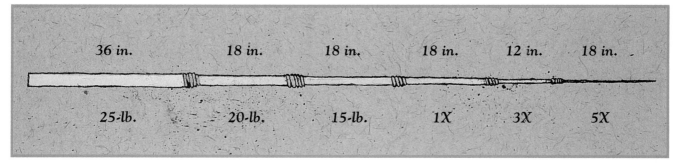

36 in.	18 in.	18 in.	18 in.	12 in.	18 in.
25-lb.	20-lb.	15-lb.	1X	3X	5X

TROUT – A 10-foot leader for trout in moving and still water. For wary fish, add a section of 6X to 8X tippet.

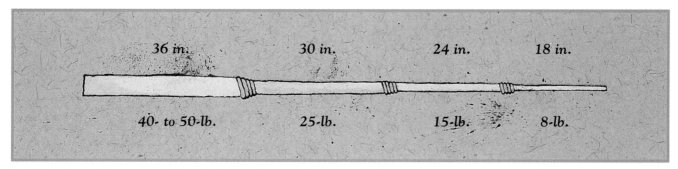

36 in.	30 in.	24 in.	18 in.
40- to 50-lb.	25-lb.	15-lb.	8-lb.

BASS – A quickly tapering 9-foot leader with a stout butt section for turning over heavy or wind-resistant flies.

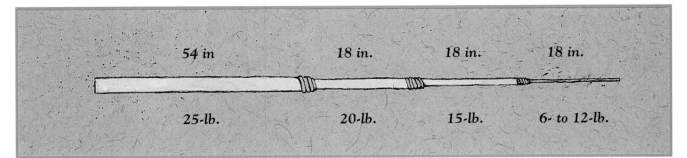

STEELHEAD – *This 9-foot leader tapers gradually and uses an extra-long butt section for turning over large flies.*

PIKE/MUSKIE – *This 9½-foot leader has a wire shock tippet for toothy pike and muskie.*

LIGHT SALTWATER – *A strong, simple 10-foot leader for species ranging from bonefish to redfish.*

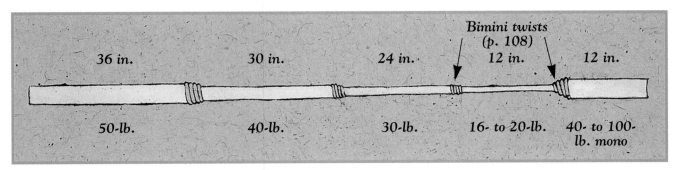

HEAVY SALTWATER – *A stout 9½-foot leader with a section of heavy shock tippet for tarpon, sailfish and tuna.*

Clothing

VESTS are the most common article of fly-fishing clothing. A standard vest (above) allows you to carry all the gear you'll need for a day on the water.

The right apparel keeps you comfortable in any weather and makes you less visible to the fish. Here's what to look for:

VESTS. A good vest should be lightweight, yet large enough to fit over a sweater or heavy shirt and hold your gear. One that feels bulky or heavy when empty will be tiring to wear when fully loaded. Some vests have an internal support strap to help distribute the weight of your gear evenly across your shoulders, and a padded collar to reduce the strain on your neck.

When choosing a vest, look for one with an assortment of pockets in various sizes for carrying accessories. The pockets should close securely with zippers or Velcro® to keep small items from falling out.

The vest should also have a large zippered pocket in the back for storing lightweight rain gear; several rings for tying on small items, such as a squeeze bottle of floatant; and a ring at the back of the collar to hold a landing net.

A SHORTY VEST (above) keeps your accessory pockets dry when deep wading. A vest with mesh panels (right) will help keep you cooler in warm weather.

Other handy features include a fleece or foam patch for drying flies before putting them in their box, and extended zipper tabs on the pockets, for easier opening with cold or gloved fingers.

If the weather is too warm for a vest or you only need to carry a small amount of gear, consider alternatives to a vest such as a chest or fanny pack, or a lightweight shirt with a number of oversize pockets.

A good chest pack should secure around your torso, as well as your neck, to keep the pack from swinging from side to side as you walk or wade.

ALTERNATIVES to vests include a fanny pack (above) and chest pack (left).

31

POPULAR HATS include: (a) baseball-style cap with long visor; (b) flats hat, with fold-down flaps for protecting neck and ears from sun; (c) full-brim hat, for shedding rain; and (d) stocking cap for cold weather.

HATS. Even on overcast days, you need a hat with a brim to reduce glare and make it easier to spot fish. Hats made especially for fly fishing often have a brim that is dark on the underside to further reduce glare.

The most popular type of hat is the baseball-style cap. Lightweight and comfortable, these caps come with visors of various lengths to shade your eyes. But they do not shade your ears and neck.

Flats-style hats have a back flap that folds down to shade your neck and ears. A full-brim hat sheds rain and helps protect the back of your head from fly hooks. Avoid brightly colored hats, especially white ones, which could spook wary fish.

RAIN GEAR. It pays to carry an inexpensive plastic rain shell or poncho in your fishing vest. This way, you're prepared for an unexpected rain shower. If you know you'll be fishing in rainy conditions, wear more substantial rain gear.

A lightweight jacket made with a breathable material, such as Gore-Tex®, can be worn all day without overheating. But some breathable materials are very expensive.

Traditional waxed or oiled cotton provides good protection, but it is expensive, weighs more than plastic or breathable rain gear and is too bulky to stash in your vest.

BREATHABLE rain gear allows moisture from perspiration to escape, keeping you dry on the inside.

Although heavy and bulky, rubber rain gear provides the ultimate in rain protection. Worn over insulating layers, it will keep you dry and warm.

WADING JACKETS. A good wading jacket is your best bet for extended foul-weather fishing because it combines the waterproof qualities of a raincoat with the short length and large pockets of a vest. Some jackets include neoprene cuffs to keep out water and a drawstring hood designed to fit over most hats.

GLOVES. Fingerless gloves made of wool, fleece or neoprene keep your hands warm even when wet, and still allow you to tie knots and grip the fly line. Choose a pair that fits snugly without restricting finger dexterity.

WADING JACKETS are a must in foul weather. Choose one that fits comfortably over a sweater, fleece jacket or other insulating layers.

FINGERLESS GLOVES are ideal for handling fish, fly line and leaders in cold weather.

33

Dressing for the Conditions

For the fly fisherman, dressing for the elements can be as important as choosing the right fly. Salmon and steelhead fishermen, for instance, often spend hours wading icy water in frigid weather. Without the right clothing, they risk hypothermia. When fishing in cold weather, dress in layers of synthetic materials that wick moisture away from the body, and wool or other insulating materials that keep you warm even when wet. Layers can be easily shed, if the weather changes.

In hot weather or tropical sun, be sure to keep your skin covered with thin, light-weight clothing to prevent burning. Long pants and long-sleeved shirts are recommended. Always use a waterproof sunblock with an SPF rating of 15 or higher on any exposed skin.

FLY-FISHING CAMOUFLAGE

Wary species like trout flee for cover at the slightest flash of color or movement. The secret to successfully stalking fish is not alerting them to your presence before you've had a chance to make a cast to them.

One of the best ways to avoid giving yourself away is to blend in with your surroundings. In most freshwater situations, drab colors such as greens and browns (top right) give you the necessary camouflage for fishing along streamside vegetation. Avoid bright colors, such as white or yellow, which can spook fish.

In saltwater situations, where the only background may be sky, choose clothing in shades of light blue and white (right) to break up your profile.

Accessories

Y ou couldn't possibly carry every accessory and gadget sold at your fly shop – nor do you always need them. Your selection depends on the type of fishing you'll be doing. Following are the most common and useful items:

FLY BOXES. Important for storing, organizing and protecting your valuable flies, boxes come in many sizes and styles for different kinds of flies. A good fly box should be light-weight, hold your flies securely without crushing them, close tightly to keep out moisture and fit easily in a pocket of your fly vest. Popular fly-box styles include:

Compartment. This style is ideal for storing dry flies, which have delicate hackle that can crush easily. Some have compartments with individual, see-through lids that keep flies from blowing away or falling out

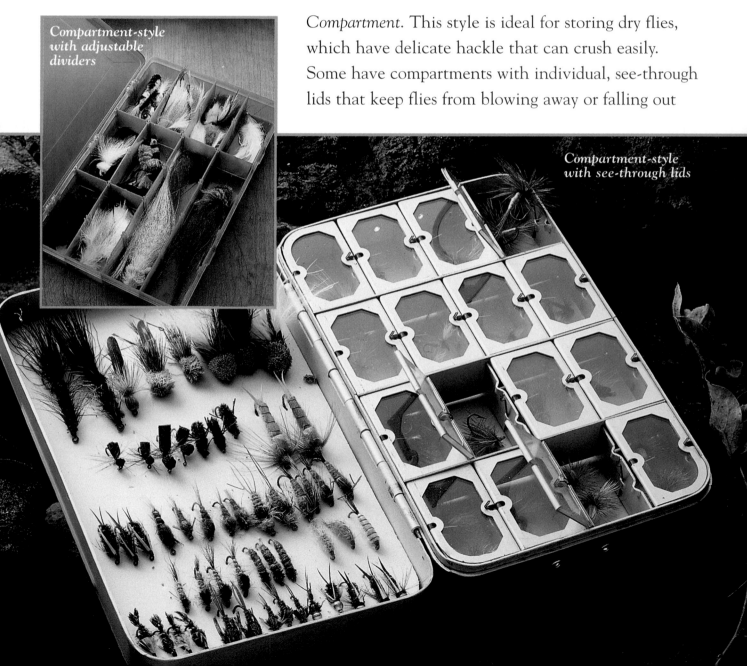

Compartment-style with adjustable dividers

Compartment-style with see-through lids

when you open the box. Others have a single lid with movable dividers that let you adjust the size of the compartments to suit your flies. Be careful not to overfill the compartments; this will crush the flies.

Foam-lined. Inexpensive and lightweight, this style comes in flat and ripple foam, or a combination of the two. Flat foam is adequate for all but dry flies with delicate hackle. Ripple foam is better suited for dry flies. Hook them so the hackle falls in front of the ridges.

Clip. This classic style is used for storing wet flies, particularly salmon and steelhead patterns, as well as streamers and nymphs. Most clip boxes are metal; as a result, they tend to be heavy and more expensive than other styles. Clips should never be used to hold dry flies.

Fleece. The traditional fleece-lined wallets are attractive but have little value for storing flies. The fleece will crush the feathers on almost any fly, and a fly put away damp will rust quickly.

Magnetic. Boxes with magnetic lining are gaining popularity, but tend to be heavier than other styles. They do not hold dry flies well because the hackle keeps the magnet from gripping the hook.

WEIGHTS. Several types of weights will help you get your fly down to the fish. These include:

Split Shot. By far the most common style, split shot comes in both lead and nontoxic lead substitute. Lead is softer and can be pinched securely to your leader without damaging it. Lead substitutes, such as tin, are lighter than similar-size lead shot and, because they are harder, are more likely to come off during a cast or damage your leader.

Moldable. Nontoxic tungsten compound is molded around your leader. You can easily adjust the weight, remove it and reuse it.

Twist-on. These narrow lead strips come in small spools or matchbook-style dispensers. When wrapped around a leader, they have a slim profile, making them snag-resistant. But they can damage your leader and create a "flat spot," which makes casting difficult.

Foam-lined

Clip

TYPES OF WEIGHTS

WEIGHTS include
(a) split shot,
(b) moldable and
(c) twist-on.

TYPES OF STRIKE INDICATORS

Dry fly

Yarn

Corky

Foam adhesive

Float putty

Twist-on

Fly line

STRIKE INDICATORS. Once viewed with disdain by purists, strike indicators have nonetheless revolutionized nymph fishing. Indicators make it easier to tell when a fish has taken a subsurface fly. Today, most nymph fishermen add an indicator of some type to their leader, setting the hook at the slightest twitch or pause in the indicator's drift. Styles of indicators include:

Dry Fly. One of the oldest and most effective indicators is a dry fly; the wet fly or nymph is trailed below it on a length of tippet material, called a *dropper.* Because a fish can strike either fly, this style of indicator can increase your odds of success.

Yarn. A small tuft of poly yarn tied into a knot in your leader makes an inexpensive but highly effective indicator. Poly yarn floats well, comes in a variety of high-visibility colors and can be used to create a very large, yet lightweight, indicator.

Corky. This style is threaded onto the leader and held in place with a peg, usually the tip of a toothpick. A corky is simple to reposition, but in order to remove it, you must first snip off the fly.

Foam Adhesive. These popular peel-off indicators come in large sheets. The white or fluorescent tab is secured by folding it around the leader. These indicators float well and are easy to spot on the water, but often leave adhesive on your leader when removed, and are difficult to reposition.

Float Putty. Moldable, versatile and highly buoyant, float putty can be rolled into any size or shape, is easy to affix and is reusable, but can sometimes leave a residue on your leader.

Twist-on. These indicators are easy to add and remove, float well and are highly visible. Simply place your leader into the groove in the indicator and twist the flexible rubber ends. Twist-on indicators are easier to adjust than the adhesive style.

Fly Line. One of the simplest indicators is a section of floating fly line with the core removed. Thread the section onto your leader and secure it by pulling it over a knot. These indicators are ideal for slow water, or anywhere a larger indicator may spook the fish.

DRY-FLY FLOATANTS. Most dry flies only float for a short time before they absorb water and sink, losing their effectiveness. As a result, they must be treated with some type of floatant before use, and then periodically during use. Floatants come in paste, spray, powder and liquid forms.

Silicone dry-fly floatant can also be used to treat sections of leader and fly line to help them float higher.

TYPES OF DRY-FLY FLOATANTS

PASTE. The most popular type of floatant, pastes are easy to use and very effective. Most pastes are made of silicone, which, used sparingly, floats your fly high. But silicone pastes tend to get hard in cold weather, and using too much will gum up the hackle, wings and tail. It's best to squeeze a small amount of paste into the palm of your hand and rub it around with your finger until it becomes a liquid, then apply it to the fly.

SPRAY. Available in aerosol and pump, spray floatants are commonly used to treat new, unused flies. But sprays may take several hours to dry and do not work on flies that are already wet, making them impractical for use while fishing.

POWDER. If your fly becomes waterlogged or coated with fish slime, dessicant powders or crystals will remove the moisture, allowing you to treat it again with a paste or liquid. Choose a container that allows you to place the fly into the powder, close the lid and shake the bottle to coat the fly.

LIQUID. These floatants, usually petroleum based, come in small jars. Simply dip your fly into the jar and allow it to dry completely before fishing. Liquid floatants dry more quickly than sprays and can be use on drowned flies. But the jars are quite heavy.

Forceps

FORCEPS. Also known as a *hemostat*, this medical tool is ideal for a variety of tasks, from removing small hooks to mashing down barbs. Flat-jaw forceps are better for mashing down barbs on tiny hooks than grooved-jaw. Most models lock closed, allowing you to clip them onto your vest.

ZINGER. This small, handy pin-on device contains a retractible cord that allows you to attach a variety of tools and gadgets to your vest.

THERMOMETER. Knowing the water temperature helps you predict insect and fish activity. In a typical trout stream, for instance, 52° water triggers many insect hatches. Select a small thermometer designed for use in water, preferably one with a protective case that can be attached to a zinger.

NEEDLENOSE PLIERS. You'll need needle-nose pliers to remove hooks from larger fish, mash down barbs, and cut and form wire leaders. Stainless-steel pliers are best because they won't corrode and seize up.

NIPPERS. Similar in design to nail clippers, nippers are essential for cutting line and trimming knots. They are sharper and cut more cleanly than ordinary clippers, making it easier to thread the tippet through the eye of a tiny fly. Some models have a needle for clearing head cement from hook eyes.

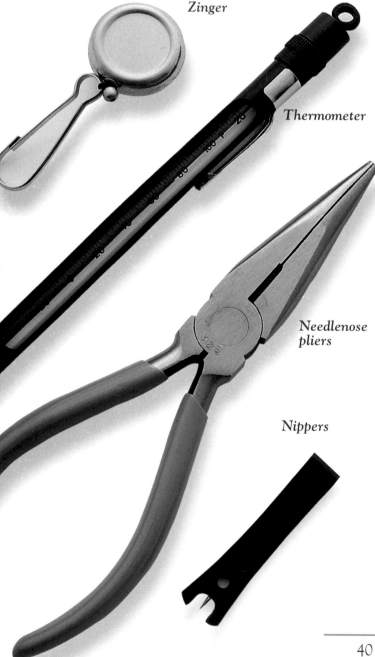

Zinger

Thermometer

Needlenose pliers

Nippers

LEADER STRAIGHTENER. A coiled leader won't lie on the water properly. When it is drawn through a rubber leader straightener, the friction creates enough heat to straighten it.

MAGNIFIERS. Even anglers with good eyesight have trouble threading small hooks or tying fine tippet material. Clip-on magnifiers attach to the brim of your hat and flip up out of the way when not in use.

LIGHT. A small flashlight can extend your time on the water. Choose a clip-on model with a flexible neck that allows you to direct the beam and work with your hands free.

HOOK SHARPENER. A small ceramic, stone or diamond-dust hook sharpener is handy for putting a point on a small hook. You may need a file for larger hooks.

TAPE MEASURE. Choose a small retractable model that clips to your vest for measuring fish.

AMADOU. This highly absorbent natural tree fungus is useful for drawing the moisture out of a waterlogged fly. Amadou is particularly good for drying flies made from cul-de-canard (CDC) feathers, which come from the oil gland area of a duck and shouldn't be dressed with floatant.

Leader straightener

Magnifier

Light

Hook hone

Tape measure

Amadou

41

Landing net

Magnetic net clip

Stripping basket

LANDING NET. A net enables you to land your fish quickly; this way, they can be released with minimal stress.

A knotless, soft-nylon net with small mesh (above) is crucial to prevent split fins and tails, which can cause infections.

Hang a short-handled net from the D-ring on the back collar of your vest using a French or magnetic clip (left).

You'll need a long-handled net for fishing from a boat.

STRIPPING BASKET. Popular for saltwater surf fishing or any type of fishing that requires handling large amounts of loose fly line, a stripping basket fastens around your waist with a belt and catches the line you strip in. This way it won't get tangled around your feet, hooked on rocks or stepped on.

Collapsible models are easy to carry and store when not in use.

Seine

Sunglasses

Bug repellent

Log book

Maps

SEINE. Use a small net to determine what insects trout might be feeding on below the water or on the surface.

SUNGLASSES. A good pair of polarized sunglasses greatly reduces glare and enables you to see fish below the surface, while protecting your eyes from errant flies. Side shields reduce glare even more. Be sure to buy glasses that block harmful UV rays.

BUG REPELLENT. Choose a solid-stick, roll-on or spray-on repellent that can be applied without getting it on your hands. Most bug repellents will quickly destroy a fly line.

LOG BOOK. Keeping a record of your fishing successes and failures can help improve your fishing. Use a log that allows you to record time, weather, location and hatch information, as well as flies used and fish caught.

MAPS. The back roads that lead to prime fishing waters usually do not appear on a standard highway map. Look for U.S. Geologic Survey quad maps, county maps or other maps with a high level of detail.

Store your maps in a clear, waterproof bag to protect them, and even if you have good maps, always carry a compass.

CHEST WADERS (above) expand your fishing range by allowing you to wade deeper. Stocking-foot waders (far left) require a separate wading boot, but are more comfortable to walk in than boot-foot waders (left), because they fit tighter and provide more ankle support. However, boot-foot waders are easier to put on and remove, and because they fit more loosely, won't restrict your circulation in cold water.

Wading Gear

Your choice of wading gear depends on the depth and temperature of the water you'll be in, how far you'll be walking and how much traction you'll need. Whatever gear you choose should fit well, keep you dry when wading and allow you to walk comfortably.

Wading gear comes in two common types: chest waders (opposite), which are best for wading in deep water; and hip boots (right), which are ideal for small, shallow streams or anywhere you are unlikely to wade deeper than mid-thigh.

Both types come in boot-foot and stocking-foot styles, and are available in a variety of materials (p. 46).

For warm-weather and saltwater fishing, some anglers prefer *wet wading*. Instead of waders or hip boots, they wear shorts or lightweight, fast-drying pants, along with wading sandals or flats boots (p. 48).

HIP BOOTS have straps that fasten to your belt to keep them up, and an internal strap system that secures the boots to your calves, so they can't slip off. Selecting boots that fit snugly at the ankle also helps keep them from pulling off, especially in sticky mud.

WADING GEAR MATERIALS

RUBBER *is inexpensive and durable, but can be heavy and baggy. Most rubber waders are not suited for wading in very warm or cold weather.*

NYLON *is economical, lightweight and comfortable in hot weather. Wear fleece or wool pants for added insulation when you're wading in cold water.*

NEOPRENE *is warm, comfortable and durable, and it provides some flotation if you fall in. Neoprene wading gear is available in several thicknesses, ranging from 3mm to 5mm. It lets you move more easily than rubber or nylon, and fits tighter for less water resistance in swift current. But neoprene is more expensive than other materials and may be too warm in hot weather.*

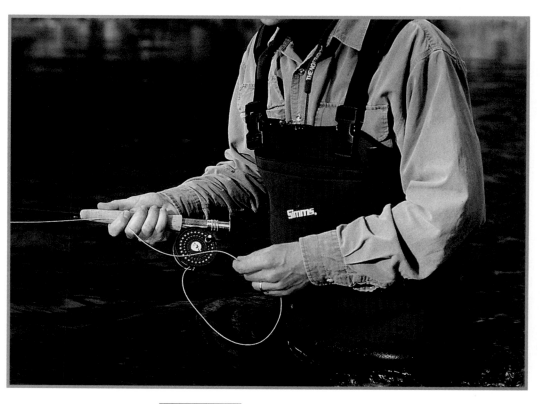

BREATHABLE materials, such as Gore-Tex®, weigh about the same as nylon but are cooler in hot weather.

Wading Sole Types

FELT SOLES provide good traction in most wading situations. They grip well on mossy rocks and in moderately fast water. Felt soles can be easily replaced if they wear out.

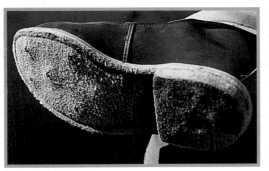

STUDDED SOLES provide maximum wading traction. They are ideal for swift or slippery-bottomed streams. The metal studs extend the life of the felt sole, as well. Strap-on cleats are also available.

LUG SOLES offer good traction on muddy banks and streambeds. They are a poor choice, however, for slippery streambeds or fast water.

WADING ACCESSORIES

A WADING BELT *should always be worn to keep your chest waders from filling if you fall in.*

A WADING STAFF *helps you keep your balance in heavy current. A folding model can be carried in a holster or your vest. Use a tether line to keep it from floating away if you drop it.*

WADING SANDALS *with felt soles are designed to be worn on bare feet or with wool or polyester socks. Use them for wet wading in warm weather.*

FLATS BOOTS, *made of neoprene with rubber soles, are designed specifically for saltwater fishing. Lightweight yet durable, they protect your feet from sharp rocks, coral, stinging fish or sea urchins.*

GRAVEL GUARDS *help prevent rocks and sand from getting into your wading boots, where they can wear a hole in your waders. They come in many styles including zippered (shown), Velcro® and elastic pullover.*

TIPS ON WADING & WADING GEAR

STAND sideways in swift current (far left) to minimize the force of the water and prevent your feet from being swept out from under you.

PIVOT upstream (left) when turning around in fast water. If you pivot downstream, the current pushes you too fast.

STAND on a plastic sheet or mat when putting on or removing waders. This prevents sharp sticks, rocks or other objects from puncturing the wader material.

HANG waders upside down in a cool, dark place, using wader hangers. Sunlight and fluorescent lights deteriorate most wader materials, and storing waders folded will cause creases that, in time, will develop leaks.

USE a wader dryer to remove all moisture before storing waders for any length of time.

Tubes & Boats

FLOAT tubes (opposite) are small, one-person watercraft consisting of an inflatable bladder with a seat in the center. They are lightweight and easy to carry (inset), and ideal for exploring small ponds and lakes. You propel the tube with kick fins (below), leaving your hands free for casting.

Whether you fish small farm ponds, vast saltwater flats or swift western tailwaters, a tube or boat can open new fly-fishing frontiers and allow you to reach waters inaccessable by wading.

Small, personal watercraft, such as float tubes or kick boats (p. 52) are ideal for waters that have little or no current, and for light wind conditions.

For larger bodies of water, moving water or carrying passengers and gear, consider larger craft such as canoes, rafts or McKenzie boats.

Powerboats, such as jonboats, bass boats and flats boats, allow you to fish waters you couldn't otherwise reach.

KICK boats are one-person, pontoon-style craft propelled with kick fins. They come in rigid-hull models, which are durable and easy to rig and transport (inset); and inflatable models, which are compact when deflated. Some have oars for covering water more quickly.

ACCESSORIES FOR FLOAT TUBES AND KICK BOATS

KICK FINS are essential for propelling float tubes and kick boats. Most fit over boot- and stocking-foot waders. Scuba-style kick fins (shown) are much more effective than side-flap or other styles that propel you forward but not backward.

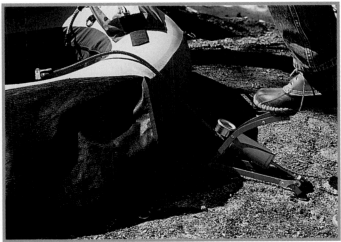

AIR PUMPS for inflating a tube or boat include: 12-volt electric (left), which can be plugged into a car's cigarette lighter; and foot-operated (above), which is inexpensive and portable.

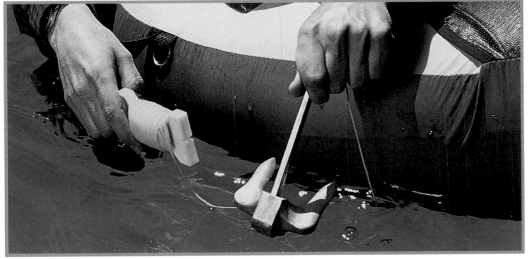

ANCHOR your tube or boat in position when fishing in the wind. Small anchors designed for tubes will allow you to work a spot without expending energy.

CANOES *are good all-around craft for day trips or extended backcountry travel. They carry a large amount of gear, but most are too unstable to stand in while casting. For maximum stability, choose a wide-beam model, preferably one with a flat, keelless bottom for maneuverability. Square-sterned canoes can be fitted with a small outboard.*

INFLATABLE RAFTS are a good-choice on swift rivers. Highly stable, they are better suited for navigating whitewater than most other types of fishing craft.

MCKENZIE BOATS *are stable and highly maneuverable, making them ideal for swift rivers. Because of their widely flared shape, only a small fraction of the hull is in the water, meaning that they move easily with a stroke of the oars. Most Mac boats have wood or fiberglass hulls, which are sturdy and quiet. Knee braces in the bow provide enough support so you can stand safely while casting.*

FLATS BOATS *are specially designed for inshore saltwater fishing. A small elevated platform allows the guide to spot fish while poling the boat, and the raised bow deck makes for tangle-free casting.*

Flies

Most traditional fly patterns are *imitators*, simulating natural foods eaten by gamefish. Practically all freshwater fish rely heavily on aquatic insects at some time in their life, explaining why so many flies used in fresh water are insect imitations. The diet of most saltwater fish, however, leans heavily toward crustaceans and baitfish, so saltwater flies usually mimic these food types.

Some imitators are painstakingly realistic, with antennae, jointed legs and other body parts that closely match those of the natural in every respect. But that degree of imitation is seldom necessary to fool a fish; in most cases, an *impressionistic* fly, one with the general look of the natural, will do the job equally well. When choosing an imitator, consider:

SIZE. Your fly should closely match the size of the natural. An imitation that is too large, even when presented well, is likely to spook the fish.

COLOR. You can't go wrong with a fly that's similar in hue to the natural. If you can't match the color, select a fly similar in shade. If the fish are taking a light-colored mayfly, for instance, don't use a dark-colored imitation.

TYPES OF FLY PATTERNS

IMITATORS *include Damselfly Nymph (top) and Olive Scud (bottom)*

SEARCHING *patterns include Adams dry fly (top) and Pheasant Tail Nymph (bottom)*

ATTRACTORS *include Royal Coachman dry fly (top) and Parmachene Belle wet fly (bottom)*

SHAPE. A fly with the general profile of the natural may be all it takes to convince the fish to bite. When the fish are selective, however, pay closer attention to tail length, wing size and body shape.

ACTION. The overall look of a fly is normally more important than its action. But there are times when action will trigger strikes. A fly with a marabou body, for example, may present a closer imitation of an undulating leech than does a fly with a hair body.

TEXTURE. Texture does not entice a fish to take a fly, but it may affect how long the fish holds onto the fly. A spun-deer-hair bug, for instance, feels more like real food than a hard-bodied bug, so a fish may mouth it for an instant longer before rejecting it, giving you more time to set the hook.

Often, you'll see insects hatching sporadically, but you won't be able to spot a predominant hatch. This is the time to try *searching patterns*, flies that represent a broad spectrum of insect life, rather than a specific insect form.

Some flies, called *attractors*, bear no resemblance to any kind of natural food. They rely on bright colors, flashy materials or sound to arouse a fish's curiosity or trigger a defensive strike.

REALISM VS. IMPRESSIONISM

Lots of anglers have the mistaken idea that trout will only take a precise imitation of the natural.

But most of the time, a fish can't afford to be that selective. If he's holding behind a rock and an insect drifts by, he's got to make a split-second decision on whether or not to take it.

Ninety percent of the time, the fish will take any fly that's similar in size, shape and color to the natural.

Flytiers who insist on imitating every detail of the natural are doing so to create a work of art, not to catch fish.

John Randolph

Dry Flies

When fluttering insects fill the air and rising fish dimple the water, it's time to tie on a dry fly. Designed to be fished on the surface, dry flies imitate the adult forms of aquatic insects such as mayflies, stoneflies, caddisflies and midges.

Used primarily for trout, dry flies will also take Atlantic salmon, bass and panfish.

Trout that gorge themselves when adult insects are hatching can be quite selective, explaining why tiers have created so many dry fly patterns.

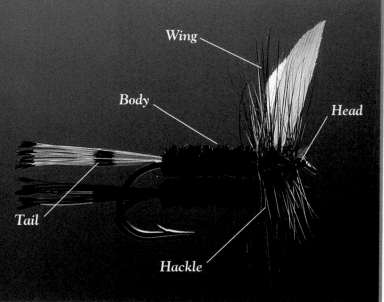

Wing

Body

Head

Tail

Hackle

DRY FLIES *are usually tied on a light wire hook for maximum flotation, and consist of the elements shown. Some are also tied with a ribbed or segmented body.*

Types of Dry Fly Patterns

Red Quill

Hemingway Caddis

UPRIGHT WING – *The most common type of dry fly, this style has wings resembling those of a live mayfly. The wings are usually made from feathers or hair.*

DOWN WING – *The wings are folded back tentlike over the body of the fly to imitate a caddis or stonefly. The wings, commonly made of hair, may also be made of feathers or thin plastic film.*

Trico Spinner

Olive Thorax

Blue-wing Olive Parachute

SPENT WING – *This type imitates a dead mayfly, which floats on the water with spread wings. Most patterns have wings of feathers or poly yarn.*

THORAX – *The wing is tied in near the center of the hook, with dubbing on each end, to create a realistic underwater image of a mayfly.*

PARACHUTE – *These flies have a single upright wing, made of hair or poly yarn, that forms a base around which the hackle is wrapped horizontally.*

Brown Bivisible

Brown No-hackle

Brown Variant

BIVISIBLE – *A wingless pattern with dry-fly hackle wrapped palmer-style along the length of the hook shank to form the body.*

NO-HACKLE – *Made with quill-segment wings, these patterns float low in the surface film to imitate an emerging adult.*

VARIANT – *Tied with oversized hackle and usually no wings, variants imitate spiders and water skaters.*

Nymphs

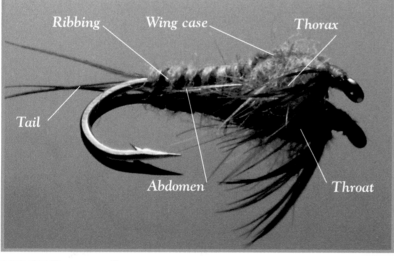

Ribbing Wing case Thorax

Tail

Abdomen Throat

NYMPHS are usually tied on heavy-wire hooks, and consist of the elements shown above. They can be weighted with lead, or lead substitute, or with a brass bead.

The term "nymph" refers to imitations of the larval, pupal and nymphal stages of aquatic insects. Some, called *emergers*, simulate an insect just prior to hatching. While adult insects are available to fish for only brief periods, these immature forms are present throughout the year and make up a much higher proportion of the diet.

Some nymphs are intended to simulate crustaceans, such as scuds, shrimp and crayfish.

Nymphs are effective not only for trout, but also for panfish and bass. They can be classified according to the type of immature aquatic insect they imitate.

NYMPH PATTERNS AND NATURALS THEY IMITATE

Mayfly Nymph

Dark Hendrickson Nymph

MAYFLY NYMPH *imitations have a wing case on the back, feathers or picked-out dubbing on the sides to represent the legs, and a feather or hair tail designed to mimic the two- or three-filament tail of the natural.*

Giant Black Stonefly Nymph

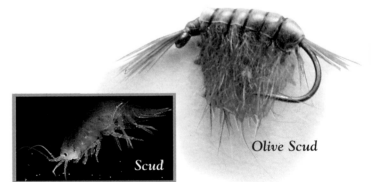

Stonefly Nymph

STONEFLY NYMPH *imitations often have antennae and two-filament tails made of goose biots or other stiff feathers. The wing case usually has two or three segments.*

Peeking Caddis

Cased Caddis Larva

Olive Scud

Scud

CASED CADDIS LARVA *imitations have legs of dark material, such as peacock herl, to imitate the natural. The body is made of yarn or dubbing, with no tail.*

SCUD *imitations, tied on short-shank hooks, have epoxy or plastic shellbacks, and legs of picked-out dubbing. Some have hackle-fiber antennae or tails.*

EMERGERS *are designed to imitate nymphs that are almost ready to hatch. The wing cases, often made of hackle-feather loops, poly yarn or a ball of dubbing, trap enough air to make the fly float in the surface film with most of the body submerged. Some patterns include a small foam ball. Emergers are tied on light-wire hooks.*

Goblin Emerger

Wet Flies

Wet flies were designed centuries ago to imitate drowned insects, and they are still effective for this purpose.

Most commonly used for trout and salmon, wet flies work equally well for panfish, especially crappies and sunfish.

Some wet flies, such as palmer-hackle or soft-hackle types (opposite) have no wings and resemble crustaceans or immature or stillborn aquatic insects. Patterns tied with tinsel and iridescent feathers have the flashy look of a minnow. Attractor patterns rely on their gaudy colors.

A typical wet fly is tied using absorbent materials such as wool or chenille to help it sink easily, and soft hackles or swept-back wings to give it a lifelike action.

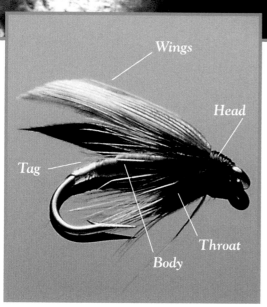

WET FLIES are usually tied on a thick wire hook and consist of the elements shown at left. Some can also incude oither elements, such as hackle wrapped palmer-style along the length of the body, or a sparse tail.

Wings

Head

Tag

Throat

Body

TYPES OF WET FLIES

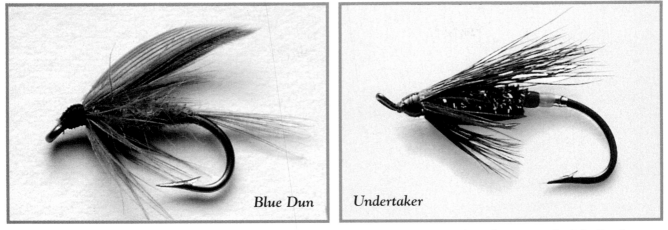

Blue Dun

Undertaker

TRADITIONAL WET FLIES are usually tied with feather wings (left) but some have hair wings (right). Feather-wing patterns, with wings made of hackle tips or quill segments, commonly imitate drowned adult insects. Most hair-wing patterns imitate baitfish. Because hair is buoyant, the hooks are sometimes wrapped with wire or they have a brass bead head to sink the fly. Less realistic, but more durable, they sink faster and have more action, especially when retrieved with an erratic motion.

Partridge-and-Yellow

Red Abbey

SOFT-HACKLE FLIES are sparsely tied, normally with a hackle collar but no wings. They sink quickly and have good action, so they make excellent imitations of immature aquatic insects or crustaceans.

Yellow Wooly Worm

Gordon

PALMER-HACKLE FLIES have hackle wound over the entire length of the body, but no wings. They resemble terrestrials, immature aquatic insects or crustaceans. Like soft-hackle flies, they work well with a twitching retrieve.

SALMON FLIES rely on their bright colors to attract fish, and are not intended to imitate real stream life. Some patterns, like the Gordon (above) are extremely intricate. Called "fully-dressed," many of these artistic creations are tied for display purposes only and never see water. Fully-dressed salmon flies are expensive because they are difficult to tie and often call for rare or exotic materials that can no longer be legally imported.

STREAMERS are usually tied on extra-long hooks and can be weighted with lead. Most consist of the elements shown at right.

Wing

Butt

Head

Body

Throat

Streamers

As freshwater gamefish grow larger, their diet generally includes fewer insects and more baitfish. This explains why streamers, which simulate baitfish, are such effective big-fish flies.

Streamers will take practically any kind of gamefish, including trout and salmon; large-mouth, smallmouth and spotted bass; white and striped bass; crappies; and northern pike, muskies and pickerel. They are also the primary saltwater fly.

Like wet flies, they are often tied using absorbent materials to help them sink. Weight, such as lead wire, is added to help reach deeper lies of large gamefish. Some streamers have realistic eyes for extra attraction, and monofilament weedguards for fishing in weeds.

TYPES OF STREAMERS

HACKLE-WING *streamers have a wing made of long, relatively stiff hackle feathers. These flies sink readily, so they can be fished fairly deep, even with a floating line. They work well in both moving and still water.*

Light Spruce

Muddler Minnow

Royal Coachman Bucktail

MUDDLERS *have large heads of clipped deer hair and wings of turkey quill segments, marabou or hackle feathers. Highly versatile, they work in still or moving water. Most muddlers float, or sink very slowly. But some are wound with lead wire, so they can be fished on bottom.*

BUCKTAIL *streamers have a wing made of bucktail, calf tail or other hair. They sink more slowly than hackle-wings, but can be fished deep with a sinking or sink-tip line. Like hackle-wings, bucktails work well in moving and still water.*

Black Matuka

Janssen Black Marabou

MATUKA *streamers have a hackle-feather wing secured the entire length of the body with thread or tinsel. This way, the wing never becomes fouled in the hook bend, as it may on a hackle-wing. The wing forms an upright keel, giving the fly good stability in fast water.*

MARABOU *streamers have a fluffy marabou wing that assumes the shape of a baitfish when the fly is wet. A marabou streamer sinks more slowly than a hackle-wing. When twitched, the fly has a pulsating action, so it works well in either still or moving water.*

Terrestrials

Whether or not a hatch is on, a trout won't hesitate to grab an ant, beetle or other terrestrial insect that drifts by. Terrestrials work equally well for bass and panfish, and they're just as effective in still water as in streams.

Terrestrial imitations are a good choice in summer, when winds blow large numbers of land insects into the water. But these flies are an option any time the naturals are available.

Tied with buoyant materials so they float high on the surface, terrestrials can be twitched to mimic the struggle of a live insect.

TYPES OF TERRESTRIALS

Dave's Cricket

HOPPER AND CRICKET *imitations often have feather wings and jointed legs. Tied on long-shank hooks, in sizes 6 to 14, they work best in late summer.*

ANT *imitations have a segmented body and are tied on standard-length hooks, usually in sizes 14 to 20. These flies are effective throughout the season.*

Black Fur Ant

Black Beetle

BEETLE imitations can be year-round producers. Most have a deer hair or foam shellback and are tied on standard-length hooks, usually in sizes 12 to 18.

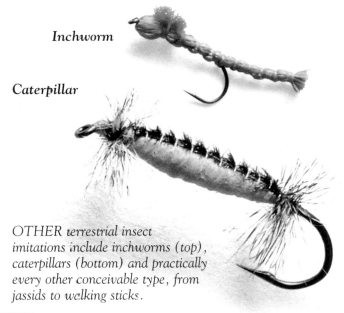

Inchworm

Caterpillar

OTHER terrestrial insect imitations include inchworms (top), caterpillars (bottom) and practically every other conceivable type, from jassids to walking sticks.

Bugs

A smashing surface strike ranks as one of the most exciting moments in fishing. But excitement is not the only reason for using these topwater flies. Few other lures work as well when fish are feeding on surface foods like large insects, frogs or mice.

But bugs can be effective even if you don't see fish feeding on the surface. They work particularly well for many warm-water species during the spawning period and are a good option whenever fish are in the shallows.

These flies range in size from the inch-long sponge bugs used for panfish to the 10-inch divers used for pike and muskies. Because of their weight and wind resistance, these large flies can be difficult to cast, so many are tied with lightweight materials, such as clipped deer hair, marabou and synthetic materials teased to appear bulkier than they really are.

While most bugs imitate some type of real food, some attract fish mainly by the surface disturbance.

TYPES OF BUGS

Chug Bug   Hair Popper   Bass King

POPPERS have a cupped or flattened face that produces a popping sound when the fly is twitched. They have bodies of foam, clipped deer hair, cork or balsa wood, often with hackle collars, hair or feather tails and rubber legs.

DIVERS imitate frogs or wounded minnows. They are similar to poppers, but the top of the head slopes back, causing them to dive when pulled forward. As they submerge, most divers gurgle and emit an air bubble. On the pause, they float back toward the surface.

Dahlberg's Mega Diver

SPONGE BUGS have a soft body, so fish will hold them longer than they will hard-bodied bugs. Most have rubber legs and resemble terrestrials. Used primarily for panfish, sponge bugs float low on the water or ride just beneath the surface.

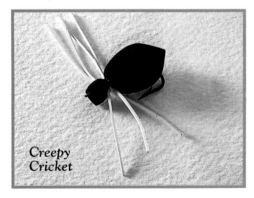

Creepy Cricket

Hard-bodied Slider

SLIDERS. Because of their bullet-shaped head, sliders cause less surface disturbance than poppers, so they work better for spooky fish. You can skitter them over fast water or slip them over dense surface cover. The streamlined shape makes them easier to cast in the wind.

REALISTIC BUGS include mouse imitations (right) and frog imitations (far right). You can also find flies tied to simulate large insects and practically any other kind of food a good-size gamefish is likely to eat.

Mouserat

Whit's Wiggle-leg Frog

Specialty Flies

Specialty flies do not fit in any of the usual fly categories, but they work extremely well in a variety of specific fishing situations.

When smallmouth bass are gorging themselves on crayfish, for instance, a crayfish imitation works better than a streamer or any other kind of fly. Similarly, nothing can top an egg fly when rainbows are feeding heavily on the roe of spawning salmon.

Types of Specialty Flies

Clouser's Crayfish

Dave's Crayfish

CRAYFISH FLIES have feathers, tufts of hair or other material tied to imitate the pincers of a crayfish. They work well for crayfish feeders like smallmouth bass, spotted bass and large trout.

LEECH FLIES have a long tail made of marabou or a strip of chamois or rabbit fur, giving the fly an undulating action similar to that of a leech. These flies appeal mainly to bass, panfish and trout.

Black Leech

Chamois Leech

Single Egg   **Egg Cluster**   **Krystal Egg**

EGG FLIES are used mainly for steelhead, salmon and trout. These simple flies are tied with fluorescent material to imitate a single egg or a cluster of eggs drifting with the current. They can also be tied with white hackle to imitate a spermed egg.

Saltwater Flies

These flies are tied to mimic some element in the diet of a saltwater fish, ranging from tiny shrimp to foot-long baitfish.

Saltwater flies are generally tied on stainless-steel hooks, so they won't corrode. And they're made with durable materials that will withstand strikes by fish with powerful, toothy jaws.

The aggressive nature of most saltwater fish makes them susceptible to extremely fast retrieves. Many saltwater patterns are tied with the hook point riding up; this way, they won't foul or hang up when stripped rapidly across the bottom.

Many patterns used in fresh water work just as well in salt. A Dahlberg Mega Diver, for instance, is intended mainly for big northern pike and muskies, but is also highly touted for striped bass, redfish, bluefish and even tarpon.

TYPES OF SALTWATER FLIES

Bonita Candy

Clouser's Deep Minnow

Lefty's Deceiver

Skipping Bug

FISH IMITATIONS are much like freshwater streamers, with a large wing made of hair, feathers or synthetic materials such as Fishair or Flashabou. Most patterns have glass, plastic or painted eyes. These flies vary in size from inch-long patterns for bonita to foot-long patterns for marlin.

Popovic's Ultra Shrimp

McCrab

CRUSTACEAN PATTERNS represent a wide variety of shrimps and crabs. Many are very realistic, with epoxy or silicone shellbacks. Because they are fished on the bottom, most patterns are tied with the hook point riding up or have a mono weedguard. These flies are most popular for bonefish, permit, redfish, weakfish and corbina.

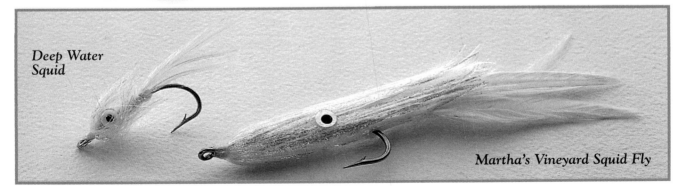

Deep Water Squid

Martha's Vineyard Squid Fly

SQUID PATTERNS have a long tail, usually made of feathers, to imitate the tentacles of the natural. The glass eyes, lead eyes or plastic doll eyes, which are placed far back on the body, also give these flies a squidlike look. Squid patterns are an excellent choice for stripers, bluefish, tuna and bonita.

Matching the Tackle to the Fish

It would be nearly impossible to cast a size 3/0 diver intended for pike with the same outfit you'd cast a size 24 mayfly imitation for brookies. The rod and line would simply not have the power to propel such a heavy, wind-resistant fly. Although it's not necessary to buy a different fly-fishing outfit for each type of gamefish you pursue, you'll be able to make better casts and enjoy your fishing much more with one that is designed to handle the flies you're casting and the fish you're after.

Although fly size is an important factor in determining the right outfit, give equal consideration to the type of water you're fishing, the distance you're casting and conditions that could impair your casting. If you're fishing a wide river and making long casts under windy conditions, for instance, it pays to use a heavier rod than you would for fishing a narrow creek with brushy banks.

On the pages that follow are tackle and fly recommendations for each important category of freshwater gamefish, along with guidelines for selecting saltwater gear.

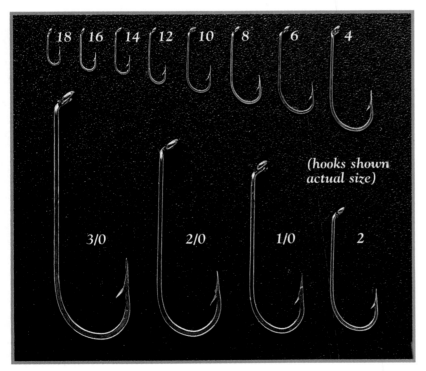

(hooks shown actual size)

HOOK SIZES for the majority of fly patterns range from size 18 to size 4. Larger hooks, from size 2 to 6/0, are used for streamers, bugs and specialty flies. Hooks smaller than size 18 are needed for tiny mayfly and midge imitations.

THE PERFECT ALL-PURPOSE FLYROD?

Eventually, every fly fisherman asks: "Can I get one fly rod that will do everything for me?" That depends on what is meant by "everything." If you will be fishing for, say, trout and nothing else, the answer could be yes. However, if you want to fish for many different kinds of fish on rivers, lakes, ponds and oceans, you will probably need a number of fly rods.

The all-purpose fly rod can be likened to an all-purpose golf club. It's possible to play 18 holes of golf with a putter, but it's certainly not efficient (and not much fun).

Tom Rosenbauer

from the
ORVIS FLY-FISHING GUIDE

Equipment for Trout

Of all the fly-rod species, trout present the greatest angling challenge. Not only can they be highly selective in their feeding habits, the wide range of waters they inhabit requires a variety of fishing techniques, and thus, fishing equipment. The best outfit for fishing tiny dry flies in a small mountain stream, for instance, wouldn't be a good choice for nymphing a big river.

The wide variety of fly sizes used for trout also dictates different tackle. Although there are times when the biggest trout in the stream will take the smallest fly in your box, those times are the exception. Smaller trout tend to be insect eaters; big trout, fish eaters. So fly size and weight of tackle tend to increase with the size of the trout. On the following pages are recommendations for a light trout-fishing outfit and a heavy one, along with a good selection of flies to use with each.

LIGHT TROUT

For many trout anglers, the challenge of coaxing a wary 10-inch brown from a brushy, clearwater spring creek is greater than landing a 10-pound rainbow in a broad Alaskan river.

Small-stream enthusiasts rely on short rods, light lines and tiny flies for the skillful presentations these fish demand. For them, a rod that's capable of delivering a fly with pinpoint accuracy at 20 to 30 feet is more important than one that will cast an entire line.

SMALL TROUT FLIES

Henryville Special

Blue-wing Olive Parachute

Adams

Trico Spinner

Olive No-hackle

Griffith's Gnat

Flying Ant

Renegade

Brassie

Serendipity

Pheasant Tail Nymph

Prince Nymph

HEAVY TROUT

You'll need heavier tackle for casting big, wind-resistant flies and powering good-sized trout out of fast current or dense cover. Big trout are usually found in big water, and this type of tackle also helps make the long casts necessary to reach the fish and to punch the line into a strong wind.

If you want to buy a single outfit that will work for most trout fishing, consider a 9-foot, 6-weight rod, with balanced reel and line. Although it may not be ideal for casting the tiniest mayfly patterns or the biggest streamers, it will do the job in most trout-fishing situations.

EQUIPMENT TIPS FOR TROUT

SPREAD a leader-sink compound on your tippet when trout are extra-spooky. A sunken tippet is less visible, especially in flat water, and casts less shadow than a floating one.

USE forceps to hold a tiny dry fly by the hook bend when tying it on. This way, you won't crush the hackle with your fingers, and you can easily twist the fly to tie a clinch knot (p. 98).

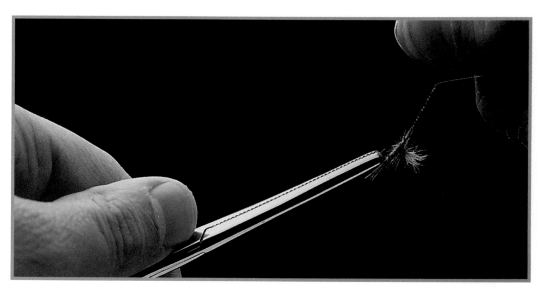

Royal Wulff

Yellow Humpy

Dave's Hopper

Hellgrammite

Giant Black
Stonefly Nymph

Bead-head
Hare's Ear

Mickey Finn

Light Spruce

Llama

Olive Whit's
Sculpin

Black Marabou
Muddler

Lead-eyed Egg
Sucking Leech

Equipment for Steelhead and Pacific Salmon

Steelhead and salmon returning from a life at sea swim hundreds of miles up their native streams to reach the precise spot where their life began. In addition to streams along the Pacific coast, steelhead and salmon now inhabit many inland waters, particularly the Great Lakes and their tributaries.

Large, gaudy streamers are the best choice for coho and chinook salmon; small streamers, wet flies and nymphs, for pinks and sockeyes. Egg patterns will take any salmon, and steelhead can be caught on all of these patterns.

SUGGESTED EQUIPMENT

- *Rod/Line:*
  6- to 10-weight

- *Line type:*
  Weight-forward or shooting head

- *Leader:*
  9 to 12 feet

- *Tippet:*
  6- to 12-lb.

POPULAR FLIES FOR STEELHEAD AND PACIFIC SALMON

Single Egg

Egg Sucking Leech

Teeny Steelhead Leech

Alaskabou

Polar Shrimp

Skunk

Equipment for Atlantic Salmon

Spectacular leapers, Atlantic salmon are the fly angler's dream fish. Even their species name, *salar*, means "leaper." They reach weights exceeding 40 pounds.

Atlantics spawn in streams throughout the North Atlantic region, including Iceland, Scotland, and Russia, but nowhere are they abundant. In Quebec and the maritime provinces, for example, one fish per day is considered a good catch rate.

Two-handed spey rods, 11 to 15 feet long (below), enable you to mend line more easily and make long casts without a backcast, when there are streamside obstacles behind you.

POPULAR FLIES FOR ATLANTIC SALMON

Cosseboom

Black Dose

Lani's Waller Waker

Rusty Rat

Gold Rat

SUGGESTED EQUIPMENT

- Rod/Line:
  7- to 11-weight

- Line type:
  Weight-forward or
  double-taper

- Leader:
  9 to 10 feet

- Tippet:
  8- to 15-lb.

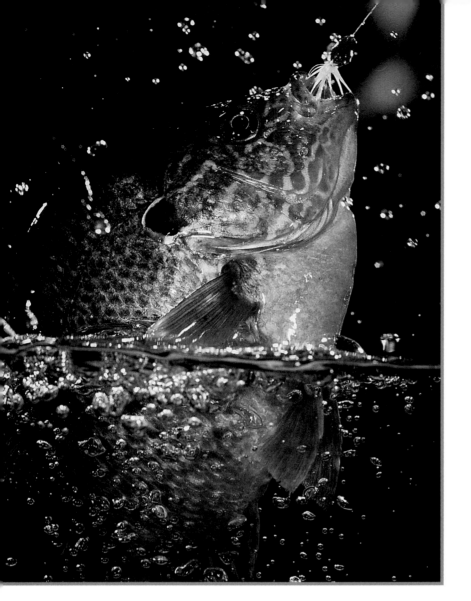

Equipment for Sunfish

If you like fast action, try tossing a popper onto a sunfish spawning bed on a warm spring evening.

Bluegills are the most surface-oriented of the sunfish. Besides poppers, they will also slurp in sponge bugs, dry flies and terrestrials. Redears, or *shellcrackers*, which feed mainly on snails, are less likely than bluegills to take surface offerings.

Most any small wet fly or nymph fished near the bottom will catch all types of sunfish.

POPULAR SUNFISH FLIES

Black Gnat

Jacklin's Hopper

Elk-hair Caddis

Mini-pop

Pan Pop

Creepy Cricket

Bead-head Hare's Ear

Pheasant Tail Nymph

Wooly Worm

Leadwing Coachmen

Equipment for Crappies

Wet flies and small streamers rank among the deadliest of all crappie lures, especially in spring, when spawners move into the shallows.

If you can see spawning crappies in the shallows, cast to the darker-colored fish, which are the males. They're considerably more aggressive than the females.

Once crappies leave the shallows, they can be difficult to find, and fly fishing is not nearly as effective.

POPULAR CRAPPIE FLIES

Black-nosed Dace

Byford's White Zonker

Muddler Minnow

Black Gnat

White Miller

Yellow Sally

SUGGESTED EQUIPMENT

- *Rod/Line:* 2- to 5-weight

- *Line type:* Double-taper or weight-forward

- *Leader:* 7½ to 9 feet

- *Tippet:* 4X to 8X

Equipment for Smallmouth Bass

SUGGESTED EQUIPMENT

- Rod/Line:
  6- to 8-weight

- Line type:
  Weight-forward or
  bass taper

- Leader
  6 to 9 feet

- Tippet
  2X to 5X

The aerial antics and line-stretching power of a big smallmouth will test the skill of any fly fisherman. Subsurface patterns, such as streamers, big nymphs, crayfish patterns and leech imitations top the list of productive smallmouth flies. When smallmouth go deep, try weighted flies or use a sink-tip line.

Although smallmouth are not quite as surface-oriented as largemouth, they'll readily take bugs around spawning time or whenever they're feeding on hatching insects.

As a rule, the flies used for smallmouth are slightly smaller than those used for largemouth.

Whitlock's
Near Nuff Frog

Sneaky Pete

Hellgrammite

Bitch Creek

Wooly Bugger

Clouser Minnow

Chamois Leech

Dave's Crayfish

Equipment for Largemouth Bass

SUGGESTED EQUIPMENT

- *Rod/Line:*
  7- to 9-weight

- *Line type:*
  Weight-forward or bass taper

- *Leader:*
  6 to 9 feet

- *Tippet:*
  0X to 4X

Nothing tops the chugging action of a bass bug for luring largemouth out of dense cover, but bugs are an excellent choice whenever bass are in the shallows. They're effective throughout the day in early season and are good morning and evening producers in midsummer.

Big streamers and specialty flies, such as crayfish and leech patterns, will take largemouth most of the year. Be sure to select a fly with a mono or wire weedguard if you'll be fishing in heavy cover.

POPULAR LARGEMOUTH FLIES

Dahlberg
Diving Bug

Bass
King

Messinger
Frog

Whitlock's Hare
Water Pup

Whitlock's
Hare Worm

Barr's Bouface

HOW TO ADD A WIRE WEEDGUARD TO A POPPER

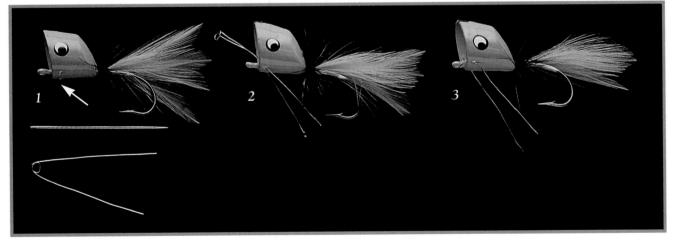

PUNCH a needle (1) through the lip of the popper on either side of the hook eye to make a pair of holes (arrow). Bend a short length of stainless steel wire (about .010-inch diameter) so it has a tight loop in the middle. (2) Push the legs of the wire down the holes. (3) Fit the loop over the hook eye, then pull the wire legs to tighten the loop. Trim the legs so they are just long enough to protect the hook point.

Equipment for Pike & Muskies

SUGGESTED EQUIPMENT

- Rod/Line:
  7- to 10-weight

- Line type:
  Weight-forward or
  bass taper

- Leader: 6 to 9 feet

- Tippet:
  8- to 14-lb.

- Shock tippet:
  12- to 30-lb.
  multi-strand
  coated wire

Landing a big pike or muskie on a fly rod ranks among the top thrills in freshwater fishing. But very little has been written on the subject, and many fly shops don't carry the right flies.

Most fly fishing for pike and muskies is done in spring, when warming water draws the hungry predators into shallow bays of northern lakes and they become easy targets for fly fishermen tossing divers, poppers, frog imitations or large streamers, including bright saltwater patterns. But some fly casters are learning that they can also catch pike and muskies along deep weedlines and on deep reefs in summer, by fishing weighted flies on full-sinking lines.

Pike and muskies respond to flashy lures, so flies tied with a little tinsel usually work best. Be sure to use flies with a stiff wire weedguard when fishing in weeds, brush or logs.

POPULAR PIKE/MUSKIE FLIES

Skipping Bug

Umpqua Swimming Baitfish

Dahlberg's Mega Diver

Lefty's Deceiver

Wool Shad

Whistler

EQUIPMENT TIPS FOR PIKE AND MUSKIE

TWIST-MELT a plastic-coated wire leader to your fly by making 5 or 6 wraps and then melting the plastic coating with a lighter. Avoid heating the plastic so rapidly that you burn the coating off the wire.

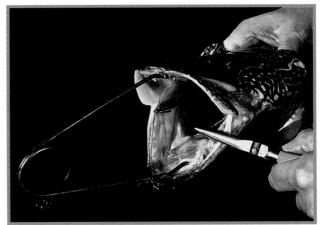

CARRY jaw spreaders and needlenose pliers for removing flies from the toothy jaws of a pike or muskie.

Equipment for Bonefish

SUGGESTED EQUIPMENT

- *Rod/Line:*
  6- to 9-weight

- *Line type:*
  Saltwater taper

- *Leader:*
  9 to 12 feet

- *Tippet:*
  6- to 12-lb.

The initial sizzling run of a bonefish explains why it ranks among the most challenging fly rod species. If you touch the spinning spool or don't have at least 200 yards of backing, you may be left flyless.

Bonefish feed on shallow flats, usually on an incoming tide, rooting the bottom for a variety of crustaceans and divulging their location by exposing their silvery tails.

Most bonefish flies give the general impression of a shrimp. They are weighted to sink fast enough that, when cast ahead of a moving school of bones, they make it to the bottom before the fish arrive.

POPULAR BONEFISH FLIES

Crazy Charlie Tan

Crazy Charlie Pearl

Horror

Snapping Shrimp

MOE Bonefish

Popovic's Ultra Shrimp

Equipment for Tarpon

Imagine a 100-pound "silver king" cartwheeling at eye level and you'll understand why tarpon present the ultimate fly-fishing thrill.

Like bonefish, tarpon are fish of the flats. They can sometimes be seen rolling on the surface with dorsal fins exposed.

Most tarpon patterns are sparsely tied hackle-wing streamers, about 2 to 4 inches long – surprisingly small considering the size of the fish, which may exceed 150 pounds.

POPULAR TARPON FLIES

Abel's Tarpon Anchovy

Stu Apte Black Death Plus

Tarpon Orange/Yellow

Tarpon Cockroach

Huff's Ballyhoo Tarpon Fly

Equipment for Redfish

Although not as glamorous as tarpon or bonefish, redfish are gutsy fighters and excellent table fare.

Also known as "red drum," the fish are found on turbid flats from Texas to New Jersey, and are commonly taken on bulky streamers from three to five inches long. The cloudy water they inhabit and their reputedly poor eyesight explain why they prefer such large offerings.

To minimize fouling on the bottom, carry a few patterns with hook points riding up. Or, try a surface bug cast well ahead of the fish to avoid spooking them in the shallow water.

POPULAR REDFISH FLIES

Whistler

Lefty's Deceiver

Umpqua Swimming Baitfish

Clouser Minnow

Whitlock Salt Shrimp

Equipment for Striped Bass

Known for their explosive topwater strikes and powerful runs, stripers are popular with anglers along both the East and West Coasts.

Stripers are notorious nomads. One day, you'll find them tearing into schools of baitfish in an estuary, on a shallow flat or along a surf line; the next, they're nowhere to be found. But they seem to favor certain feeding areas, so once you locate a good spot, be sure to check it frequently.

Most stripers are taken on bulky streamer patterns, especially those tied with materials that "breathe" in the water. If you see stripers busting baitfish on the surface, however, don't hesitate to try a popper or skipping bug.

POPULAR STRIPER FLIES

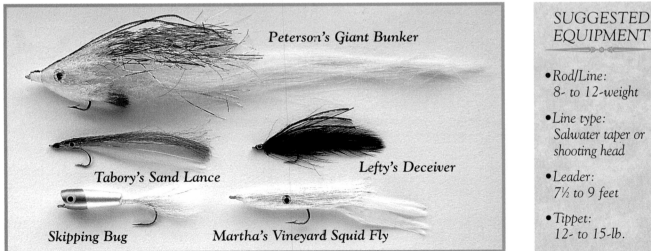

Peterson's Giant Bunker

Tabory's Sand Lance

Lefty's Deceiver

Skipping Bug

Martha's Vineyard Squid Fly

SUGGESTED EQUIPMENT

- Rod/Line:
  8- to 12-weight

- Line type:
  Salwater taper or shooting head

- Leader:
  7½ to 9 feet

- Tippet:
  12- to 15-lb.

FLY-FISHING SKILLS

Fly-Fishing Knots

In fly fishing, there can be as many as a dozen knots separating you and a hooked fish. Knowing which knots to choose and how to tie them can mean the difference between landing and losing that fish.

When tied incorrectly, monofilament line can cut through itself. An overhand knot, for instance, can reduce the strength of your leader by as much as 50 percent.

The knots that follow retain a high percentage of line strength when tied properly and are the best ones for the purposes described. For clarity, plain hooks rather than flies, and white line rather than mono, have been used in some of the knot sequences.

MOISTEN all knots before tightening. The friction caused by cinching a knot can heat the line and cause it to lose strength. Moistening your knots will reduce friction.

Attaching Backing to Reel

ARBOR KNOT

This simple knot will secure your backing so it won't slip around the spool or come off your reel if a fish takes out all your line.

1 WRAP backing around spool, and then tie tag end of backing around standing line with overhand knot. Tie second overhand knot (arrow) in tag end.

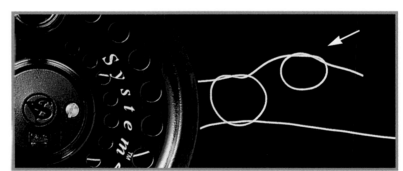

2 TIGHTEN knot in tag end and then pull standing line until knot tightens securely against arbor. Keep pulling until knot in tag end snugs up against main knot.

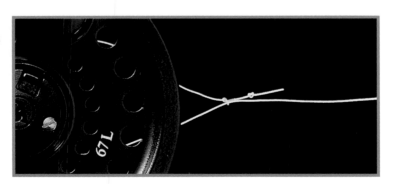

CLINCH KNOT

O̶ne of the most underrated fishing knots, the clinch knot is simple to tie, has excellent strength and can be easily undone with your fingernails. You must be careful, however, to make enough wraps so the knot won't pull out. The lighter the tippet, the more wraps you'll need. A 6X tippet may require as many as 8 wraps; a heavy shock tippet, only 3½.

1 PASS end of tippet through hook eye.

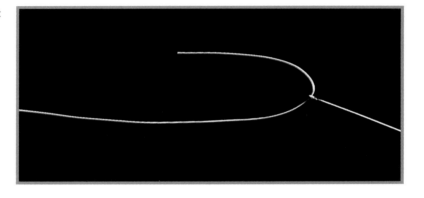

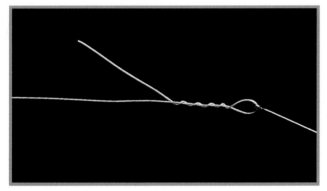

2 WIND tag end around standing line 3½ to 8 times, depending on tippet diameter.

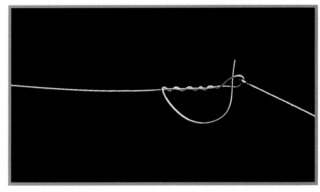

3 BRING tag end back through loop nearest hook eye.

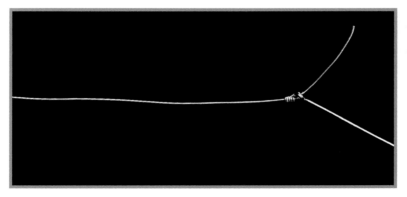

4 PULL standing line until knot is snug against hook eye. Trim tag.

DUNCAN LOOP (OR UNI-KNOT)

Among the strongest knots for attaching a fly, the Duncan loop can be snugged up with the loop open to allow the fly to swing freely, or pulled tight against the hook. The loop may close from the pull of a fish, an advantage in absorbing the shock of a hookset, but you can easily reopen it by carefully sliding the knot back.

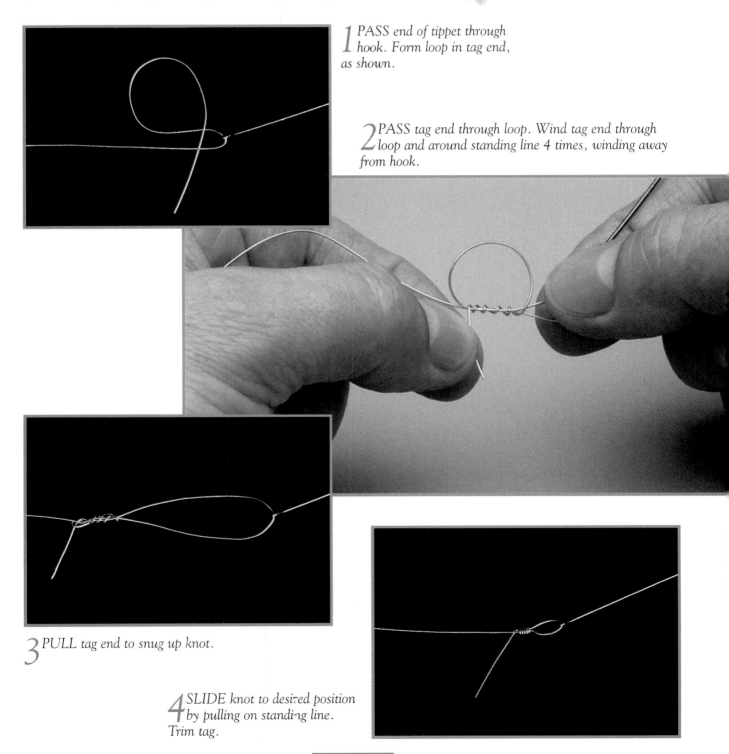

1 PASS end of tippet through hook. Form loop in tag end, as shown.

2 PASS tag end through loop. Wind tag end through loop and around standing line 4 times, winding away from hook.

3 PULL tag end to snug up knot.

4 SLIDE knot to desired position by pulling on standing line. Trim tag.

Joining Two Sections of Monofilament

DOUBLE SURGEON'S KNOT

This knot is best for joining sections of leader or tippet material that differ by more than .003" in diameter. It is easier to tie and stronger than a blood knot, but does not lay out perfectly straight.

1 PLACE two sections of line to be joined side by side, tag ends facing opposite directions.

2 MAKE a loop in double line. Pass both ends of line on right through loop to form an overhand knot.

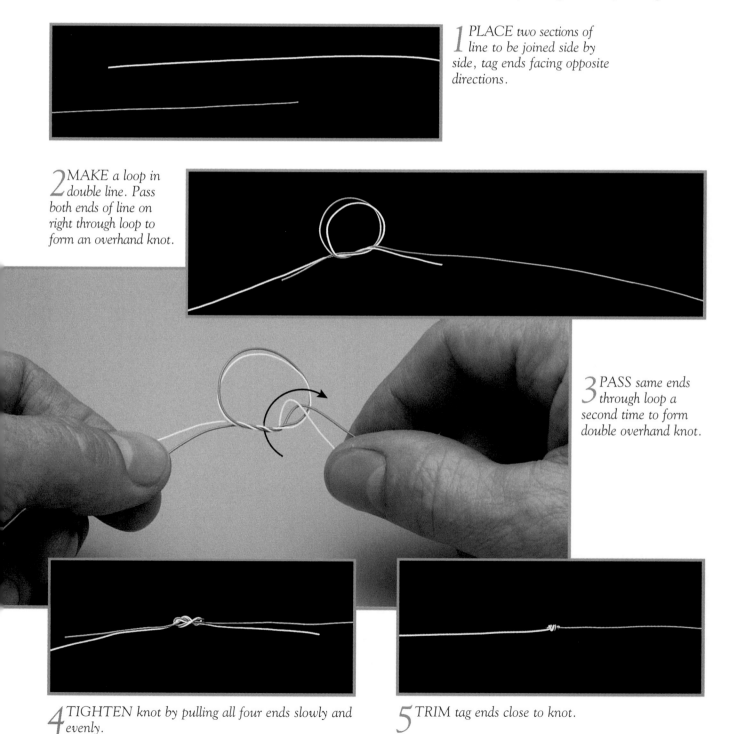

3 PASS same ends through loop a second time to form double overhand knot.

4 TIGHTEN knot by pulling all four ends slowly and evenly.

5 TRIM tag ends close to knot.

BLOOD KNOT

This knot is a good choice for joining two sections of similar-diameter leader or tippet material. It works better than a double surgeon's knot for joining long sections of mono, and forms a connection that lays out straighter.

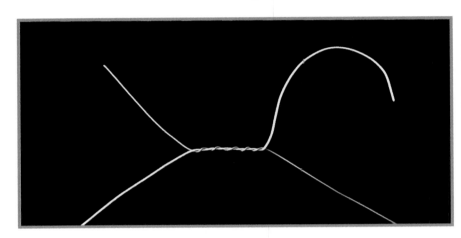

1 CROSS the two sections of line to be joined, and then wrap one tag end around standing part of other line 5 to 7 times, depending on line diameter.

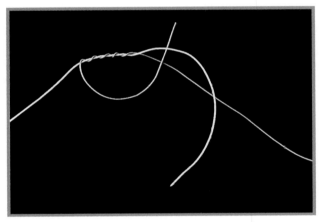

2 PASS tag end back between the two lines.

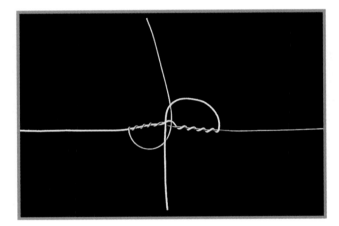

3 WRAP other tag end around other standing line 5 to 7 times. Pass tag through same opening as first, in opposite direction.

4 PULL standing lines to tighten knot. Trim tags closely.

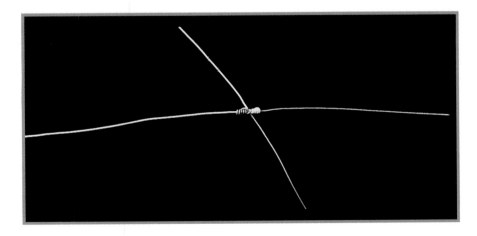

Making a Loop in a Leader

DOUBLE SURGEON'S LOOP

This is the simplest knot for making a loop in either end of a leader. The loop can then be attached to a loop in the fly line or another leader section with a loop-to-loop connection (p. 107).

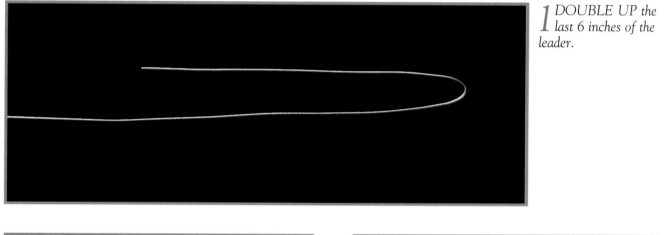

1 DOUBLE UP the last 6 inches of the leader.

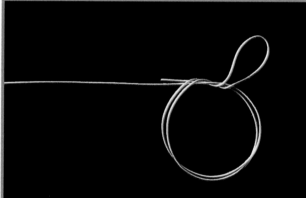

2 MAKE a loose overhand knot in double line.

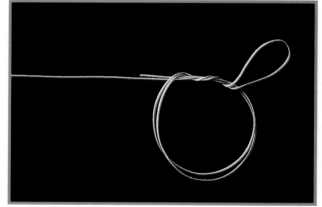

3 PASS loop end through knot a second time to form double overhand knot.

4 TIGHTEN by holding loop while pulling standing line and tag end until snug. Trim tag closely.

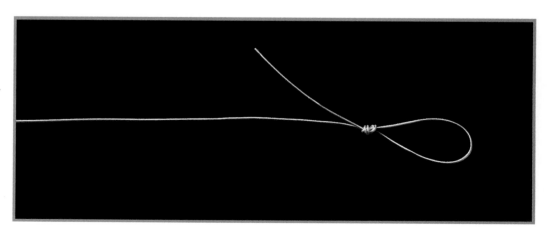

PERFECTION LOOP

Although the perfection loop is more difficult to tie than a surgeon's loop, it forms a more compact knot that is equally strong.

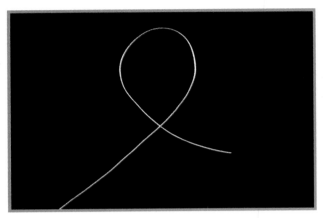

1 FORM a loop in leader by passing tag end behind standing line, tag facing right.

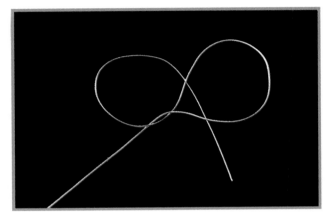

2 FORM a second loop in front of first by passing tag end around and then behind first loop.

3 PASS tag end between first two loops; hold tag end to left side.

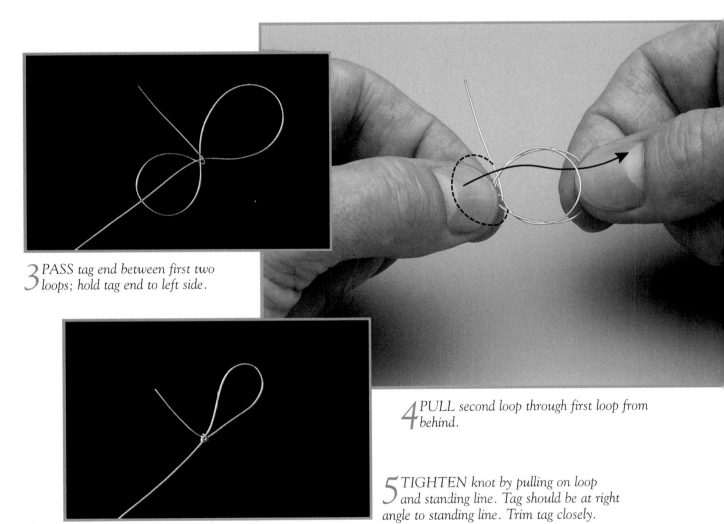

4 PULL second loop through first loop from behind.

5 TIGHTEN knot by pulling on loop and standing line. Tag should be at right angle to standing line. Trim tag closely.

Joining Fly Line to Backing or Leader

ALBRIGHT KNOT

The Albright knot is easier to tie than the tube knot, but is bulkier because the fly line is doubled. The Albright can also be used to attach a shock leader to a Bimini twist (p. 108).

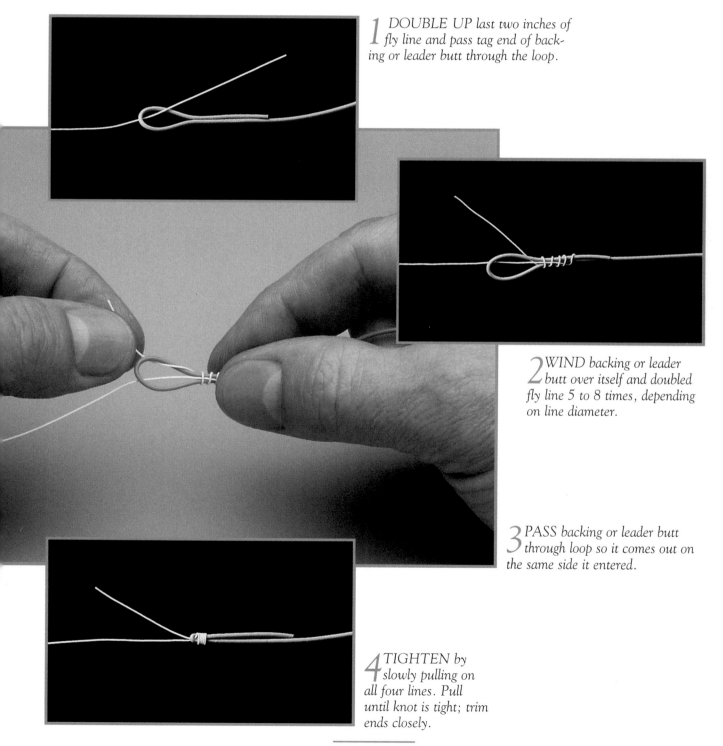

1 DOUBLE UP last two inches of fly line and pass tag end of backing or leader butt through the loop.

2 WIND backing or leader butt over itself and doubled fly line 5 to 8 times, depending on line diameter.

3 PASS backing or leader butt through loop so it comes out on the same side it entered.

4 TIGHTEN by slowly pulling on all four lines. Pull until knot is tight; trim ends closely.

TUBE KNOT

Because the tube knot is not as bulky as the Albright, it is a better choice for attaching leader butt to fly line.

1 PLACE *hollow tube alongside fly line, and loop butt end of leader alongside tube, as shown.*

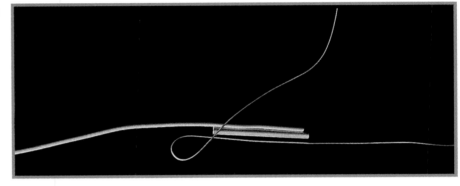

2 WRAP *butt end around tube, fly line and standing part of leader 5 to 6 times.*

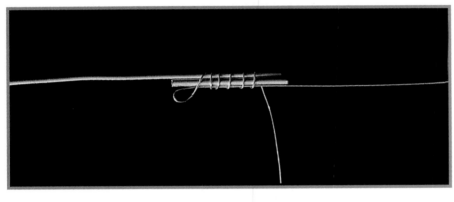

3 PASS *butt through tube as shown. Carefully remove tube. Pull tag end and standing part of leader until knot is just snug.*

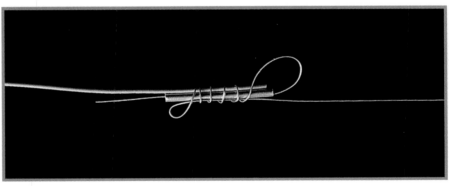

4 TIGHTEN *knot slowly, using your fingernails to position wraps evenly before tightening completely. Closely trim tag ends.*

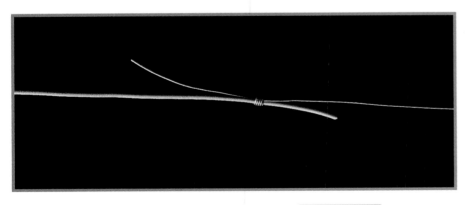

Making a Loop in Your Fly Line

BRAIDED-LOOP CONNECTOR

A braided-loop connector slips over the end of your fly line. Then, you can easily attach your leader using a loop-to-loop connection (opposite). Be sure to buy a connector that matches the size of your fly line.

Although braided-loop connectors are handy, some experts believe they hinge too much on the cast, so the leader does not roll over properly. And they may not be strong enough for big-game fishing.

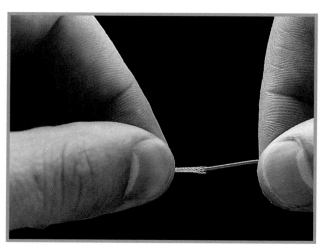

1 SQUEEZE end of connector to open braids; insert end of fly line.

2 WORK fly line into connector by alternately squeezing the braids and pushing on the line. Continue until line is as far into connector as possible; it must be in at least 2 inches to be secure.

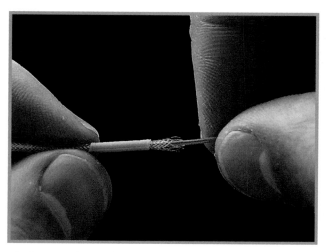

3 SLIDE plastic sleeve that comes with connector down to cover the braided end, which may be frayed.

4 DAB Super Glue® on the connector, if desired. Because the connector operates on the "Chinese finger trap" principle, however, this step is usually unnecessary.

Joining Loops

LOOP-TO-LOOP CONNECTION

Use the loop-to-loop connection for joining several leader sections or attaching your leader to a braided-loop connector (opposite). This way, you can change leaders or leader sections quickly and easily.

1 PASS loop in first section (white) through loop in second section (blue).

2 THREAD other end of second section through loop in first.

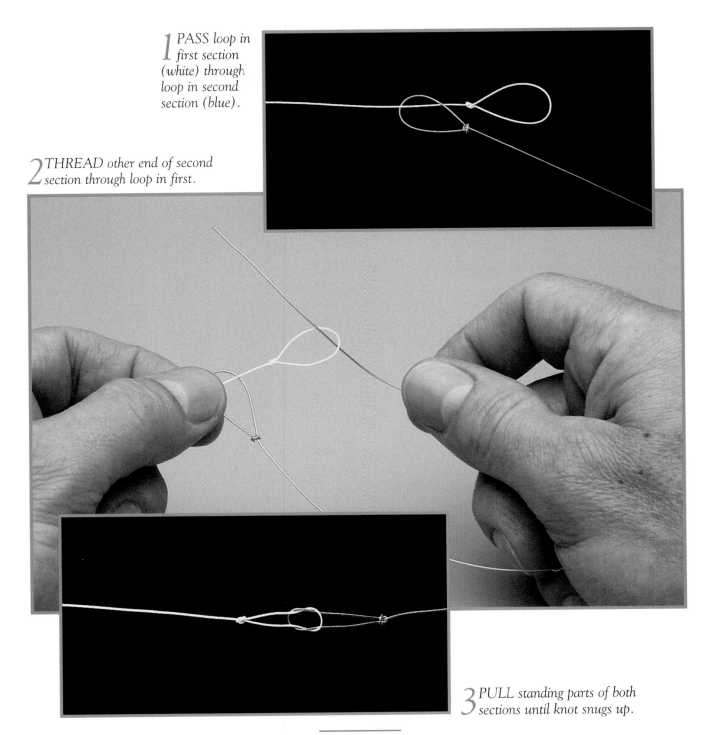

3 PULL standing parts of both sections until knot snugs up.

Making Double-line Connections

BIMINI TWIST

Popular among saltwater anglers, the Bimini twist is used in saltwater leaders (p. 29) to make strong double-line connections for attaching a tippet between the leader and shock tippet. Sometimes called the "twenty-times-around knot," the Bimini ensures that the connection is 100% the breaking strength of the tippet material, which is the weakest link.

First, tie a Bimini in each end of the tippet. Next, double one Bimini, forming a 4-line section; then make a double surgeon's loop, which attaches to the leader with a loop-to-loop connection. Attach the other Bimini to the shock tippet using an Albright knot.

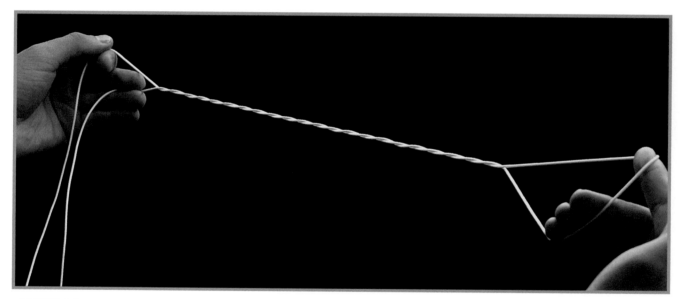

1 FORM loop in line. Place hand in loop and make 20 twists.

2 PLACE loop over knee. Hold one end of line in each hand. Spread hands to compress twists.

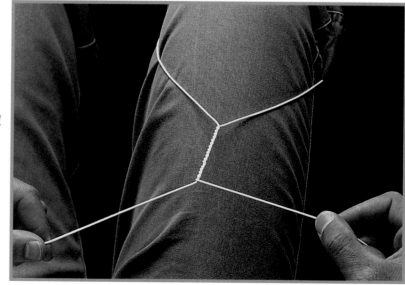

3 HOLD *tag end at right angle to twists. Pull gently upward on standing line with left hand. Tag end should begin to wrap over twists. Be sure each wrap is even and touching the previous wrap.*

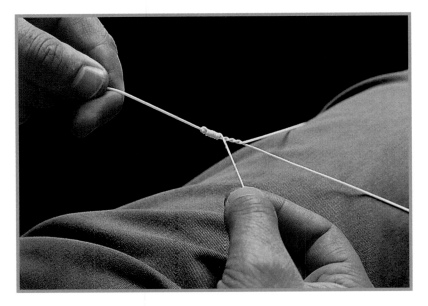

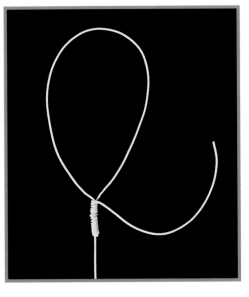

4 CONTINUE *pulling until entire twist section is over-wrapped.*

5 TIE *half-hitch around one leg of loop to prevent knot from unraveling. Tighten half-hitch snugly.*

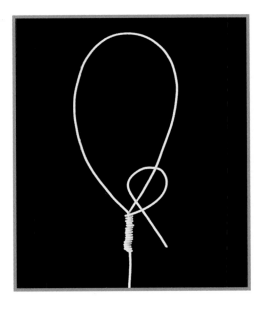

6 TIE *half-hitch around both legs of loop. Wrap tag end through half hitch and around both legs two more times, as shown.*

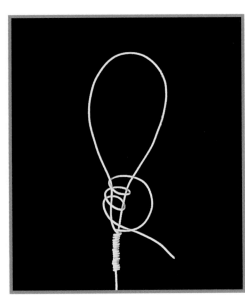

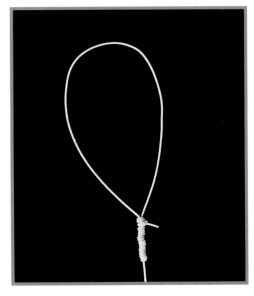

7 PULL *tag end slowly to snug up knot. Tag end should be ⅛- to ¼-inch long when trimmed.*

MODIFIED HUFFNAGLE KNOT

Use this knot to connect a heavy shock tippet to a lighter leader or a Bimini twist. The knot is very strong and compact, and the two line sections lie straight when snugged tightly.

1 TIE loose overhand knot near end of shock tippet.

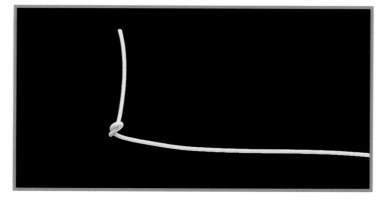

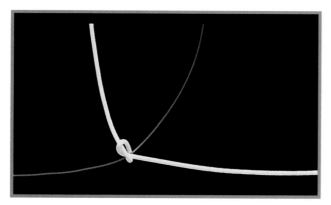

2 PASS end of leader or Bimini through overhand knot in shock tippet.

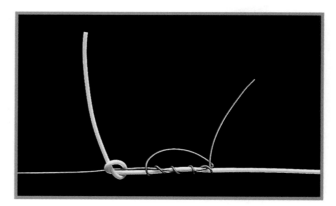

3 MAKE loop in leader or Bimini alongside shock tippet and wrap end through loop and around shock tippet 4 to 5 times, forming a uni-knot (p. 99).

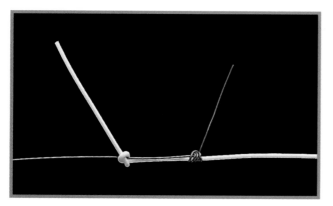

4 TIGHTEN uni-knot and overhand knot.

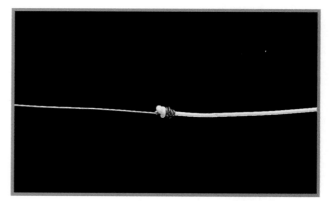

5 PULL on both lines to snug up knot; trim tags closely.

Attaching Fly to Shock Tippet

HOMER RHODE KNOT

Aheavy shock tippet restricts a fly's action, particularly when the knot is snugged up to the eye. A loop knot allows the fly to swing more freely. The Homer Rhode loop knot is easy to tie, even in heavy mono.

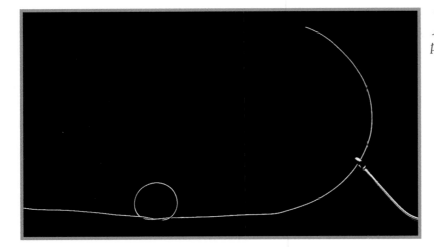

1 TIE loose overhand knot about 6 inches from end of shock tippet; pass end through hook eye.

2 PASS end through overhand knot.

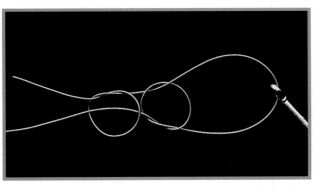

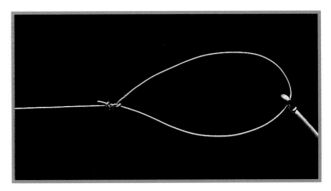

3 TIE an overhand knot with tag end around standing line. The position of second overhand knot determines size of loop.

4 TIGHTEN both overhand knots, then pull firmly on standing line until two knots slide together and snug up.

Fly Casting

The skill of accurately casting a weightless fly forms the foundation of fly fishing. Because the fly must land delicately without alarming the fish and give the illusion of life, a good cast can mean the difference between fooling the fish into taking your fly or causing it to flee.

In fly fishing, the line, rather than the lure, provides the necessary casting weight. The line, in turn, propels the leader and fly to your target.

Learning to cast a fly line is more difficult than other types of casting, but the basics can be learned in just a few hours. Smooth, accurate fly casting comes with time and practice. Before you attempt to fish, practice the basic overhead cast (p. 120) until you are comfortably throwing line about 25 to 40 feet – the distance at which most fish are caught.

Fly casting does not require great strength. Today's high-modulus rods generate higher line speeds for greater casting distance with less effort than did early bamboo and fiberglass rods.

In the past, most fly-casting instruction was based on the clock-face method, with the fly rod representing the hour hand of an imaginary clock and the casting motion performed overhead between the 10- and 2-o'clock positions. This technique worked fine for short to medium casts, but made learning to cast longer distances more difficult.

Modern fly-casting instruction divides the casting motion used in both the forward and backcasts into three basic elements: the acceleration, the speed stroke and the stop

(pp. 116-117). Separating the casting motion into its individual parts helps you understand the mechanics of a cast, so you can cast more effectively. How you execute the elements of a cast is more important than where on the face of a clock.

Once you have mastered the basic elements, apply them to perfect the overhead cast and then to practice false casting, distance casting and roll casting. If you can perform these casts, you can tailor your casting to handle almost any fishing situation.

Getting Started

HOW TO STRING THE ROD

FORM loop in fly line. Thread loop through guides and out tip-top, and then pull leader through tip-top. Doubled fly line is easier to thread than fine tippet and won't slip back through guides if you accidentally let go.

HOW TO HOLD THE ROD

GRIP rod in casting hand with thumb on top of grip, as shown. Keep rod butt in line with fore-arm, and wrist straight. The thumb helps control the rod, for a straight casting stroke, and helps support the rod when applying power to the cast.

TWO METHODS FOR GETTING LINE OUT ON THE WATER

METHOD 1. Pull entire leader through tip-top, along with 8 to 10 feet of line. Shake rod tip back and forth in front of you as you pull, or strip, line off reel. This method can be used in moving or still water.

METHOD 2. Strip several feet of line off reel. Allow current to take line down-stream. Continue to strip and feed line into current until you have fed out desired amount.

Tips for Practicing Fly Casting

No one becomes an expert fly caster overnight. It may take years of practice to perfect the skill of placing the fly precisely where you want it under various conditions. But fly casting is hardly a chore; many fly fishermen spend hours practicing just for the pleasure of throwing a fly line. Before attempting to fish, practice casting over grass to a fixed target (below). Never use a fly on the end of your leader when practicing on grass.

CHOOSE *a practice surface of water or grass (left) with no trees nearby to interfere with your line. Avoid casting over surfaces such as gravel or asphalt, which can damage your line.*

PRACTICE *accuracy, which is usually more important than distance. Use a paper plate or plastic hoop as a casting target. Position targets at various distances and practice placing the end of your leader onto each target.*

TIE *a piece of fluorescent yarn to the end of your leader in place of a fly. The yarn won't snag, is safer than a sharp hook and helps you see the end of your leader in the air and on the ground.*

The Elements of a Casting Stroke

Fly casting consists of a series of simple rod movements: the acceleration, the speed stroke and the stop. Each of these elements is necessary to complete any cast and, when combined, form a smooth casting stroke.

The step-by-step sequence shown on these pages demonstrates this basic casting stroke, but is not intended to represent a complete cast. On an overhead cast (p. 120), for instance, these elements must be performed on both the forward and backcast.

The result of a good casting stroke is a tight loop, which reduces wind resistance and focuses the energy of the cast toward your target. A poor casting stroke causes an open loop, increases wind resistance and results in a cast that is likely to fall short of its target.

Practice these basic elements on both the forward and backcast, until you master the casting stroke. Then, use this stroke in learning to make an overhead cast.

THE ACCELERATION

ACCELERATE *gradually and continuously throughout this phase of the casting stroke (backcast shown). As in throwing a ball or swinging a golf club, you must apply speed slowly, building to the next element, the speed stroke (opposite, top). This gradual application of speed helps you begin to focus the energy of the cast in the direction you want the line to go. Some casting instructors compare it to moving a paint-filled brush along the same plane as your cast: too much speed too soon will splatter the paint over a wide arc; slow acceleration keeps the paint on the brush until you are ready to release it by stopping the brush in the direction you want the paint to go.*

THE SPEED STROKE

APPLY *a short burst of speed at the end of the acceleration phase to bend, or load, the rod. When combined with an abrupt stop (below), the speed stroke helps form a tight loop. The shorter the speed stroke, the tighter the loop will be. Some instructors call it the "wrist snap" or "power stroke," but these terms are somewhat misleading. Too much movement of the wrist at any phase of the cast will throw unwanted slack into the line, opening up the casting loop; and little power is needed to perform a good speed stroke. Instead, think of the speed stroke as the "hurry-up" before the "wait" of the stop.*

THE STOP

STOP THE ROD *suddenly at the end of the short speed stroke, causing the rod to straighten, or unload, quickly. This transfers the energy from the rod to the line, forming a tight loop and propelling the line. Even with a poor acceleration and speed stroke, stopping the rod crisply will form a tight loop and cause the line to unroll smoothly. Many beginning fly casters fail to stop the rod quickly enough, resulting in poor loops. Practice stopping the rod with the tip high on both the back and forward casts; the line will travel in the direction the rod tip was moving when you stopped the rod.*

The Casting Plane

The casting plane is the path of the rod tip, and thus the line, as it travels back and forth in the air. Although commonly called a "plane," the casting plane is really just an imaginary line.

But to give you the tightest loops and most efficient casts, this line must be as straight as possible. In other words, the path of the forward cast should be in line with that of the backcast. To accomplish this, your forearm and wrist should also be moving on a straight path, *not* pivoting at the elbow. Picture the motion that would be needed to pound nails in

THE CASTING PLANE

KEEP *your casting plane level on most types of overhead casts.*

TILT *the casting plane forward to raise your backcast when there is a high bank or brush behind you.*

opposite sides of a door frame with a two-headed hammer, and use this same straight back-and-forth motion in your casts. If your forearm and rod tip travel in an arc, rather than a straight line, your casting loop will open up.

The casting plane is not always parallel to the ground. In situations where there is an obstruction behind you, tilt your casting plane forward to lift your backcast above it (opposite).

When casting sidearm to avoid overhead obstructions, such as overhanging limbs, or to keep from spooking fish in clear water, many anglers find it more difficult to maintain a straight casting plane, because their wrist and elbow tend to pivot. But the path of the line is just as important for maintaining tight loops in sidearm casting as it is in overhead casting. Watch the path of your line as you cast until you develop a feel for the arm motion needed to achieve a straight casting plane.

LOWER your casting plane from overhead to sidearm to avoid overhanging limbs (left). But keep the path of the rod tip and flyline straight (right), to maintain a tight loop.

119

The Overhead Cast

The overhead cast is used to pick up the fly line and lay it back down in order to reposition the line, leader and fly on the water. This basic and essential cast forms the foundation of many other fly-fishing casts. A fly angler may perform this cast dozens of times in a single hour of fishing.

Use the overhead cast for short to middistance casting on moving and still waters.

1 BEGIN *by letting out the desired amount of fly line in front of you (p.114). Stand facing your target with your feet spread comfortably apart. Position your rod hand so the tip of the rod is pointing in the direction of your target, with your rod, forearm and wrist aligned. Lower your rod tip and remove the slack from the line.*

2 RAISE *your rod and begin to accelerate slowly and continuously, until entire fly line is off the water.*

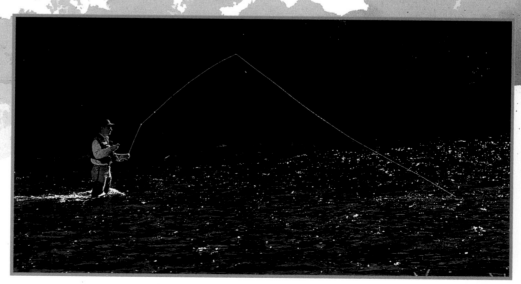

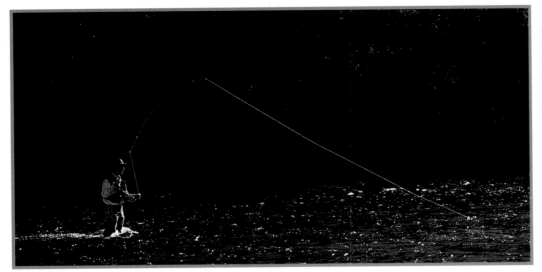

3 APPLY a short backward speed stroke, forcing a bend in the rod and generating the energy necessary to propel the line into the backcast.

4 STOP the rod crisply. A loop will form in the line as it moves overhead. The shorter the speed stroke and straighter the casting plane, the tighter the loop will be.

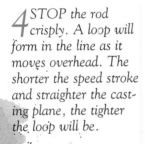

5 PAUSE as the backcast unrolls behind you. When the line unrolls to only a small "J" in the air, begin your forward acceleration.

6 APPLY a short forward speed stroke and immediately stop the rod (shown). Aim your cast about eye level above your target. Let the line settle to the water, while lowering the rod tip to the fishing position.

The False Cast

The false cast begins the same as the overhead cast, with a simple backcast and forward cast. But the false cast differs from the overhead in that the line is not allowed to settle to the water following the forward cast. Instead, as your line begins to straighten in front, you make another backcast. You can repeat this back-and-forth motion several times, if necessary, depending on the purpose of the cast. The false cast is used mainly to change direction between casts, gauge the distance of your cast and let out fly line (pp. 124-125). It can also be used to cancel an off-target cast or dry a waterlogged fly in the air.

Timing is important during the false cast. Many fly fishermen hurry their forward casts, so they often "crack the whip" with the line, possibly breaking off the fly. When learning to false cast, turn your head and watch your backcast unroll behind you. When the line unrolls to a small "J," begin your forward cast. Applying your speed stroke too early on the backcast can also cause the fly to snap off.

Aim your forward cast higher than you would on an overhead cast. Remember that the fly line will travel in the direction that your rod tip was moving when you stopped the rod. Aiming your rod higher on the forward cast will give the line more time to unroll, and allow you to begin your backcast without the line falling to the water.

The acceleration, speed stroke and stop are as important in false casting as in other kinds of fly casting. So is the casting plane. Remember to keep the rod tip traveling in a straight line parallel to the desired path of the fly line. The forward cast should be on the same plane as the backcast. Keep your wrist as straight as possible when false casting; bending it will open your casting loops.

HOW TO FALSE CAST

1 LIFT the line off the water as you would on a normal overhead cast.

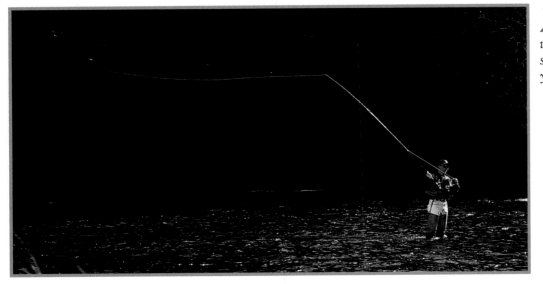

2 LET the backcast unroll behind you until the line forms a small "J." Then begin your forward cast.

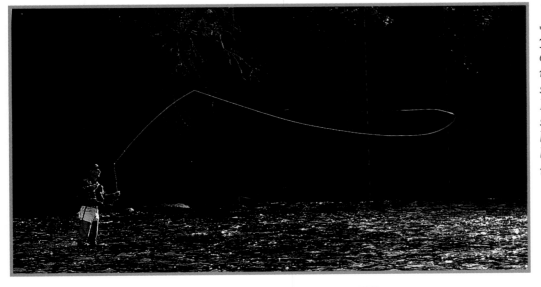

3 AIM your forward cast higher than you would on an overhead cast. Do not allow the line to settle to the water. Instead, wait until the small "J" forms in the line and begin another backcast. Repeat as necessary.

HOW TO LET OUT LINE WITH A FALSE CAST

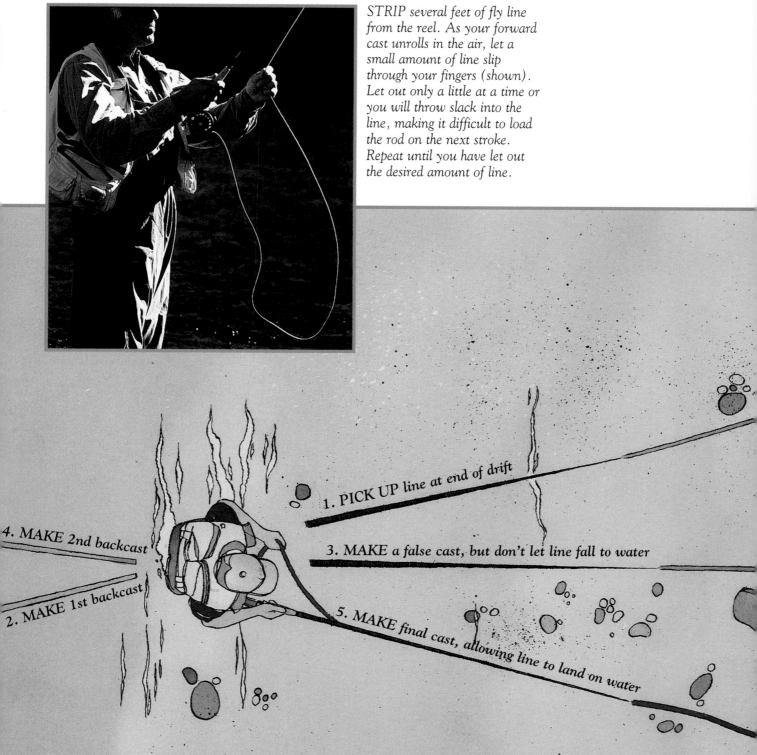

STRIP several feet of fly line from the reel. As your forward cast unrolls in the air, let a small amount of line slip through your fingers (shown). Let out only a little at a time or you will throw slack into the line, making it difficult to load the rod on the next stroke. Repeat until you have let out the desired amount of line.

1. PICK UP line at end of drift

4. MAKE 2nd backcast

3. MAKE a false cast, but don't let line fall to water

2. MAKE 1st backcast

5. MAKE final cast, allowing line to land on water

HOW TO CHANGE DIRECTION WITH A FALSE CAST

ADJUST the angle of your cast after a downstream drift by making one or more false casts until your line is directed at your target, then let the line fall to the water. Use this technique when fishing still water, as well, to change the direction of your cast from one target to the next.

How to Gauge Distance with a False Cast

MAKE *a false cast, letting the line unroll above your target, but don't let it settle to the water. Try to gauge where the fly would land. If it is short of the target, let out line on your next false cast.*

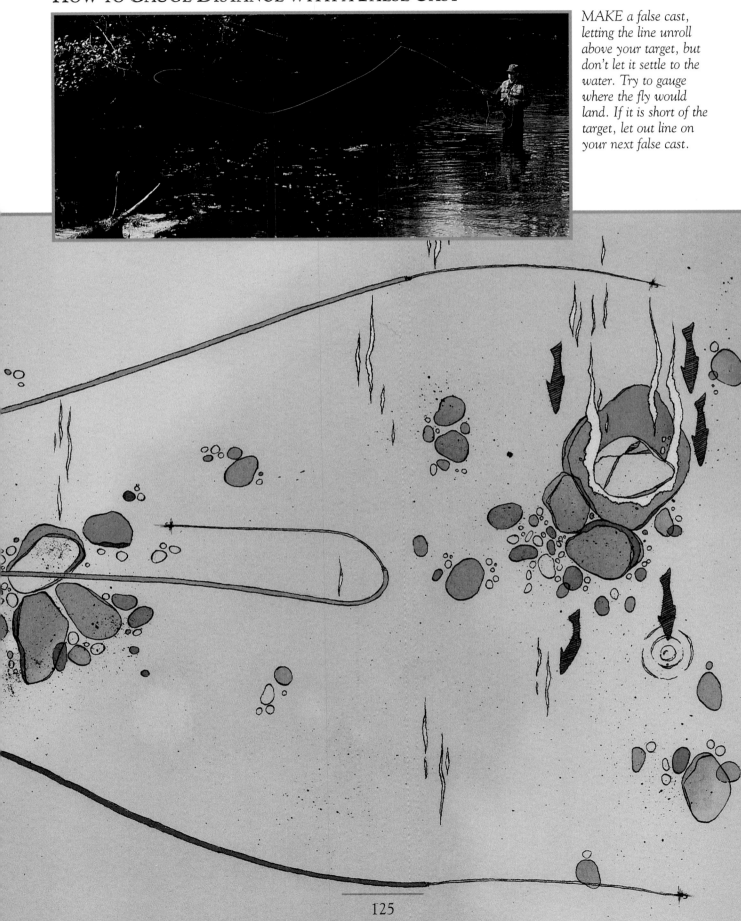

The Distance Cast

Most beginning fly casters learn to make short casts fairly quickly. But distance casting is more complicated and difficult to learn. Here are some techniques to help your distance casting.

Shooting line. This method involves making several false casts, then letting out the desired amount of line on the final forward cast (below). For hard-to-reach fish, you should learn to shoot line at least 30 feet.

Longer rod drift. Lengthening your casting strokes (opposite) gives you the extra momentum needed for longer casts. The word "drift" is somewhat misleading; it simply refers to the length of these strokes, which depends on the length of the cast. Use longer rod drift, combined with the double haul, for casting even greater distances.

The *double haul.* This technique involves making a short tug, or *haul,* on the line during the acceleration phase on both the forward and backcast (p. 128). This loads the rod more quickly, increasing line speed. Besides giving you more distance, the double haul also helps you punch the line into the wind.

HOW TO SHOOT LINE

FORM an "O" with the fingers of your line hand after you've stopped the rod. Let the forward cast pull the loose line through your fingers; the "O" will help feed the line through the stripping guide without bunching up.

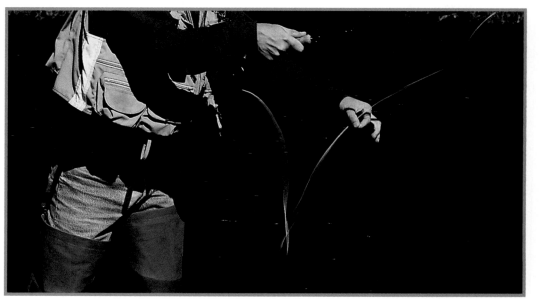

SHORT CASTS, 20 to 30 feet, require little rod drift.

MEDIUM CASTS, 30 to 50 feet, require a longer casting stroke. Stop the rod farther back on the backcast, and aim your forward cast slightly higher.

LONG CASTS, over 50 feet, require a much longer casting stroke. On the longest casts, the rod should be nearly parallel to the water at the end of the backcast. The longer the cast, the higher you should aim your line.

HOW TO MAKE A DOUBLE HAUL

1 MAKE a short, smooth downward haul, about 4 to 6 inches long, during the acceleration phase of the backcast.

2 BRING your line hand back up immediately after the haul. Let the line unroll behind you as you would on a normal overhead cast.

3 MAKE *a second haul, equal in length to the first, during the acceleration phase of the forward cast.*

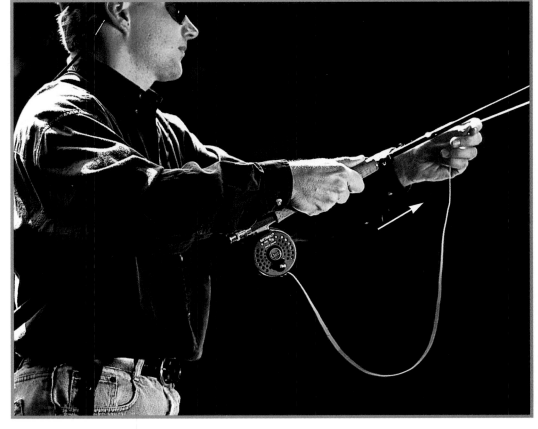

4 BRING *your line hand back up again immediately after the haul. If you are shooting line, form an "O" with your line hand instead.*

The Roll Cast

Occasionally, you'll find yourself in a situation where obstacles, such as streamside vegetation or a high bank, leave you no room for a backcast. The roll cast allows you to cast line forward without a backcast, and lets you get into tight places where you wouldn't dare risk a backcast.

Because you've eliminated the backcast, you must instead load the rod by using the friction of the water on the line (opposite). You'll need to practice this cast on the water, because grass does not provide enough friction.

Double-taper lines are easier to roll cast than weight-forward lines. The consistent diameter of the long belly transfers energy smoothly, so the line rolls out more easily.

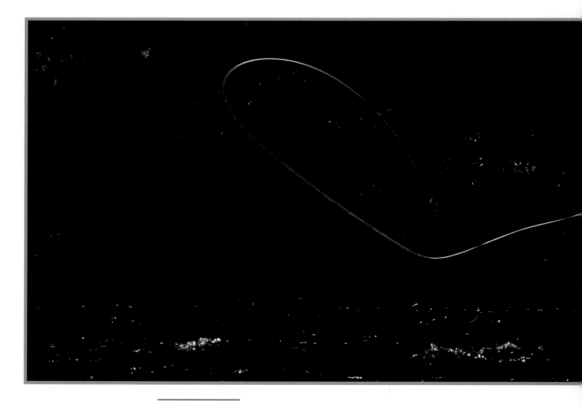

How To Roll Cast

1 LIFT *your rod tip slowly until it is slightly behind you and the line is on the water in front of you. Pause momentarily until the line stops moving toward you. This pause lets the water "grip" the line, creating enough friction to load the rod.*

2 ACCELERATE *steadily, make a short speed stroke, then stop the rod quickly.*

3 LET *the fly line roll out in front of you; it should form an elliptical loop and straighten out before settling to the water.*

Mending Line

"DRAG" & THE DRY FLY

Trout in streams seem to look for any excuse not to take a fly – even the most realistic imitation in your box. And, in most cases, that excuse is drag.

Gary Borger

Noted fly-fishing author and educator

When casting a dry fly across a current to slower water, the swifter current catches your line and forms a downstream bow. If left unchecked, this bow will pull the fly downstream faster than the current it's in, causing an unnatural wake. This phenomenon is called *drag* (photo, left). Drag can spook a wary trout and put it down for some time. The way to combat this problem is to *mend* the line, adjusting its position to eliminate drag. You can mend line in the air with the reach cast, also called an *aerial mend* (opposite), or on the water, with the *water mend* (pp. 134-135).

The reach cast lets you place the entire fly line upstream of your target as you make your cast, giving you a longer drift before drag sets in.

Another use for the reach cast to present a fly to a fish directly upstream from you without spooking it with the line. This cast allows the fly to land several feet above the fish, while the line and leader land off to one side or the other.

Water mends include two types: the upstream and downstream mend. The upstream mend is simply the technique of flipping the line upstream of your leader and fly as the line moves downstream. Unlike the reach cast, an upstream mend can be executed several times during a single drift for an even longer drag-free presentation.

The downstream mend is used when your line crosses slow water into faster water.

You can also use a water mend for controlling line in still-water situations where wind, rather than current, puts a bow in your line.

THE REACH CAST

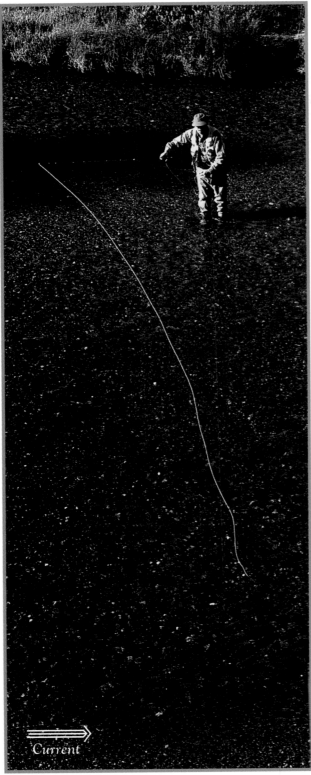

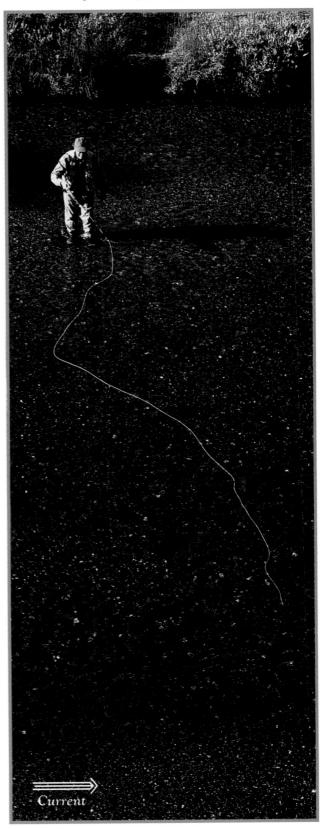

2 ALLOW *the line to settle to the water, and move
your rod to the fishing position. The line should rest
on the water upstream of your fly.*

1 STRIP *several feet of line from your reel and let it
hang free between the reel and your line hand. Make
an overhead cast. Stop the rod with the tip higher than
normal. Point the rod directly upstream while the line is
still in the air (shown), and let the slack line slip through
your line hand.*

THE UPSTREAM MEND

1 STRIP several feet of line from your reel. Allow your fly to drift downstream until just before the bow in the line causes the fly to drag.

Current

2 FLIP the line upstream with a short, semicircular motion of the rod tip (arrow, right). Let the slack line slip through your fingers as you mend, to prevent disturbing the fly. The line should settle to the water with an upstream bow (inset). Repeat as necessary.

Current

Current

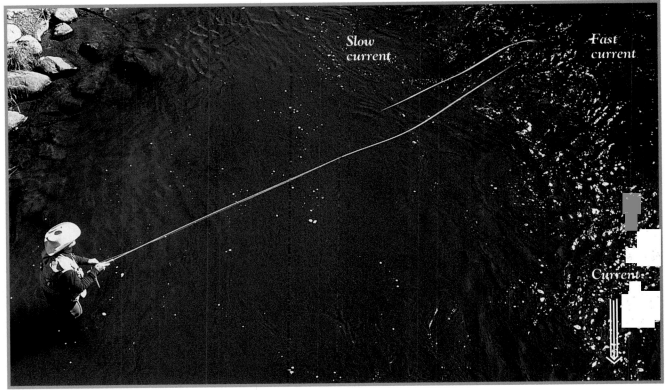

Slow current

Fast current

Current

1 MAKE a cast; let the line settle to the water. The fast current will take the end of the line downstream, while the rest of the line will form an upstream bow in the slow current. Allow the line to drift until just before the fly begins to drag.

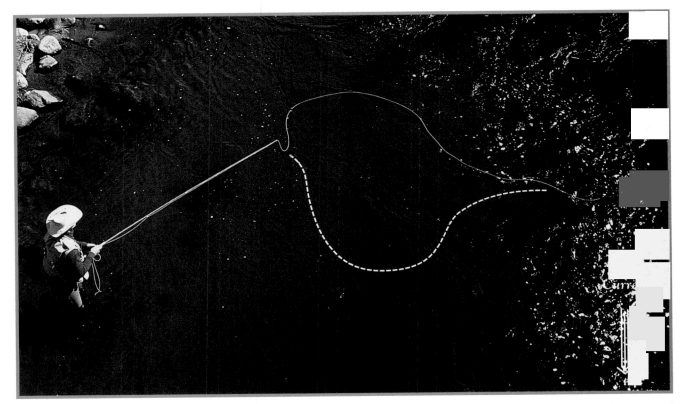

Curr

2 MEND the line downstream (dotted line) with a short, semicircular motion of the rod tip. Let out a small amount of slack line with each mend to avoid disturbing the fly.

Retrieving Line

ow you take in line is as important as how you cast it out. A
proper retrieve can give your fly action and let you control the
line as you take it in, eliminating slack for easier strike detection and
quicker hook sets.

There are two basic retrieve methods: the *strip* retrieve and the *hand-twist* retrieve. The strip retrieve (below) is best for recovering line
quickly. Use it to take up slack when drifting a dry fly or nymph in
swift water, retrieving a bass popper, or giving a streamer an erratic,
twitching retrieve to simulate the swimming motion of a baitfish.

The hand-twist retrieve (opposite) lets you take in line more slowly
and steadily than the strip retrieve, and gives you greater sensitivity
to strikes. It works well for fishing dry flies and nymphs in slow or
still water.

HOW TO MAKE A STRIP RETRIEVE

*1 HOOK line over index or middle finger of rod hand
and pinch line against rod grip.*

*2 GRASP line with other hand, pulling down while
keeping pressure on line with rod hand. Repeat until
desired amount of line is recovered.*

How to Make a Hand-Twist Retrieve

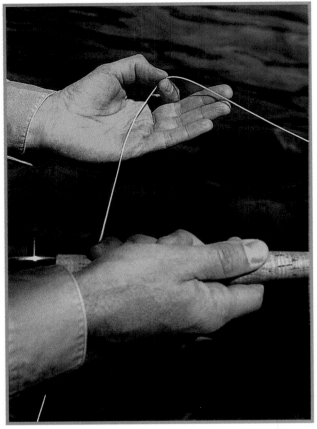

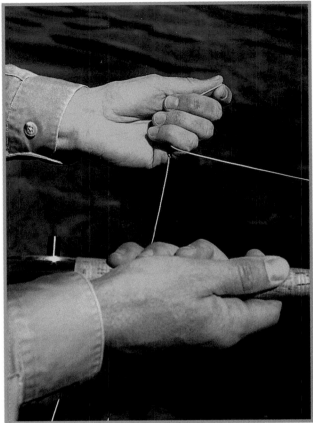

1 PINCH *line between thumb and index finger of line hand. Reach out with other three fingers to begin taking in line.*

2 GRASP *line with these three fingers and pinch line against palm of hand. Release line from between thumb and index finger.*

3 REPEAT *as necessary. Hold recovered line in palm, if desired, or allow it to fall to water as you continue to take in line.*

Glossary

Aerial mend. A mend performed during a cast, while the fly line is still in the air.

Action (rod). Term used to describe the casting performance of a fly rod. Action is determined by how and where a rod bends and how quickly it dampens.

Action (reel). Describes the rate at which a reel retrieves line.

Anti-reverse drive. A reel with a handle that turns in only one direction.

Aquatic insect. Any water-born insect, including mayflies, stoneflies, caddisflies and midges.

Attractor. A fly pattern that bears no resemblance to any kind of natural food, but instead relies on bright colors, flashy materials or sound to arouse a fish's curiosity or trigger a defensive strike.

Backing. A length of thin, uniform-diameter line, commonly braided Dacron, used to connect fly line to reel.

Belly (fly line). Portion of a fly line between the front taper and rear taper.

Blank. Term used to describe an unfinished rod.

Casting plane. The path the tip of the fly rod and, as a result, the fly line, travels in the air during a cast.

Coating. The outer portion of a fly line. The density and composition of the coating dictate a line's buoyancy; variations in the thickness of the coating determine its taper.

Core. A strand of uniform-diameter material to which fly line coating is applied. Commonly made of braided Dacron. Stiffness of core contributes to fly-line stiffness.

Dampen. To recover or cease to vibrate. Used in reference to fly-rod action.

Desiccant. Powder or crystals used to absorb water from a saturated dry fly.

Direct-drive. A reel with a handle that turns in both directions.

Disc drag. A type of reel drag that uses the smooth friction of one large surface against another to provide a braking action.

Double haul. A cast in which a haul is performed on both the forward and backcast.

Drag (fly). Any unnatural movement of an artificial fly on or below the water caused by the pull of the leader and line.

Drag (reel). Any mechanism in a reel designed to slow a running fish or prevent spool overrun.

Fast-action rod. One that bends primarily near the tip and dampens quickly.

Ferrule. Joint btween two section of a rod.

Grains. Unit of measurement used to classify weight designation of first 30 feet of a fly line.

Graphite. A strong, lightweight rod material derived from synthetic fibers subjected to high heat.

Hand-twist retrieve. Slow, steady retrieve done by grasping small sections of line in your hand.

Haul. A short downward tug on the fly line during a cast designed to increase line speed.

Head (fly line). Portion of a fly line made up of the belly, front taper and rear taper.

Imitator. A fly pattern designed to closely simulate a natural food eaten by gamefish.

Impressionistic fly. A pattern that imitates a general type of natural food, rather than a specific species.

Knotted leader. A leader made up of several sections of different-diameter line, tied end to end. Also called a "compound" leader.

Knotless leader. A single strand of leader material tapering gradually from butt to tippet.

Line tender. Elastic band used to keep fly line on reel spool from unrolling.

Load. To bend a fly rod during a cast.

Mandrel. A tapered steel form around which materials such as fiberglass and graphite are wrapped to produce a hollow rod blank.

Mend. The technique used to throw a curve into a fly line while fishing to control the drift or action of the fly.

Modulus. The ratio of stiffness to weight of fly-rod materials.

Multiplying reel. A reel with a spool that turns more than once for each turn of the handle, usually from 1.5 to 3 times.

Polyvinylidene fluoride (PVDF). A leader material, also called "fluorocarbon."

Ratchet-and-pawl drag. Type of reel drag employing the pressure of a pawl against the teeth of a ratchet to prevent spool overrun.

Recovery. How a rod dampens, or ceases vibrating, after a bend.

Rod drift. Term used to describe the length of the casting stroke. The longer the cast, the longer the rod drift.

Running line. A section of constant-diameter line that makes up the rear two-thirds of a standard weight-forward line. Also, a separate length of line attached to a shooting taper.

Searcher, or searching pattern. A fly pattern that represents a broad spectrum of insect life. Commonly used to locate fish.

Shock tippet. A section of heavy monofilament or wire between the fly and the tippet, used to protect against abrasion or breakage by toothy gamefish.

Shooting line. Method of distance casting involving letting out, or shooting, a large amount of line on a forward cast.

Shooting-taper, or shooting-head. A short, compact specialty fly line, attached to a separate running line. Used for casting very long distances.

Single-action. A reel with a spool that turns once for each turn of the handle.

Slow-action rod. One that bends over the entire length and dampens slowly.

Snake guides. Lightweight, S-shaped line guides used on fly rods.

Split cane. Another term for bamboo rod material. Commonly used to describe a rod built from slender strips of bamboo glued together.

Stripping guide. First line guide above grip on a fly rod. Generally the largest-diameter guide.

Stripping retrieve. A retrieve method in which line is pressed against grip with rod hand and recovered with line hand.

Taper (leader). Variation in thickness along length of leader.

Taper (line). Variation in thickness of a fly line's coating along its length.

Taper (rod). The way in which a rod narrows from butt to tip.

Terrestrial. Any land-born insect.

Tip (fly line). The short, level section of fly line to which leader is attached.

Tippet. The smallest-diameter section of a leader, commonly the last 10 to 25 percent.

Tip-top. Term for the guide at tip of a fly rod.

Tungsten. A dense metal compound used to add weight to fly lines. Also forms moldable lead substitute.

Water mend. A mend performed while the fly line is on the water.

Weight (fly line). A number, from 1 to 15, assigned to a fly line based on the weight (measured in grains) of first 30 feet.

Weight (fly rod). The number assigned to a fly rod, corresponding to the weight of the line the rod is designed to cast.

Wind knot. An overhand knot that forms in a tippet, seriously weakening it. Usually results from poor casting or high-wind conditions.

X-rating. Measurement of a tippet's diameter, ranging from 8X, the finest, to 0X, the thickest.

Index

Italics indicate fly patterns

A

Abel's Tarpon Anchovy, 91
Acceleration in Casting, 112, 116, 131
Accessories, 36-44
Action,
    Of flies, 57
    Of reels, 16, 17
    Of rods, 10, 11
Adams, 57, 77
Aerial Mend, 132, 133
Alaskabou, 80
Albright Knot, 105, 108
    How to tie, 104
Aluminum Fly Reels, 16
Amadou, 41
Anchoring a Float Tube, 53
Anti-Reverse Drive Reels, 16, 17
Ants, Flies to Imitate, 66, 77
Aquatic Insects, 58, 60
    See also: Insects; specific insects
Arbor Knot, 97
Ash Fly Rods, 8
Atlantic Salmon,
    Equipment for, 81
    Flies for, 81
Attractor Flies (defined), 57

B

Backing, 23
    Knot for attaching to reel, 97
    Knots for joining line and backing, 104, 105
Baitfish,
    As fish food, 72, 76, 93
    Flies to imitate, 56, 62-65, 73, 89
Bamboo Fly Rods, 9, 112
Barb, Flattening, 40
Barr's Bouface, 87
Bar Stock Reels, 16
Bass Bugs, 86
    Bass-bug taper, 20
    See also: Bugs
Bass, Flies for, 58, 60, 64, 66, 71
    See also specific bass species
Bass King, 69, 87

Bass Leader, Formula for Tying, 28
Bead-Head Hare's Ear, 79, 82
Beetles,
    As trout food, 66
    Flies to imitate, 67
Bimini Twist, 28, 104, 110
    How to tie, 108, 109
Bitch Creek, 85
Bivisible Dry Flies, 59
Black Beetle, 67
Black Dose, 81
Black Fur Ant, 66
Black Gnat, 82, 83
Black Leech, 71
Black Marabou Muddler, 79
Black Matuka, 65
Black-Nosed Dace, 83
Blood Knot, 100, 101
Blue Dun, 63
Bluefish, Flies for, 72, 73
Bluegills, Flies for, 82
Blue-Wing Olive Parachute, 59, 77
Boats, 50-55
Bonefish,
    Equipment for, 15, 29, 90
    Flies for, 73, 90
Bonita Candy, 73
Boot-Foot Waders, 44, 45
    Sole types, 47
Boots for Wading, 48
Braided-Loop Connector, 106
Braided Nylon Leaders, 25
Brassie, 77
Breaking Strength of Tippets, 27
Brown Bivisible, 59
Brown No-Hackle, 59
Brown Trout, 77
Brown Variant, 59
Bucktail Streamers, 65
Bugs, 68
    For specific fish, 84, 92
    Specific patterns, 69
Byford's White Zonker, 83

C

Caddisflies, Flies to Imitate, 58, 59, 61, 82

Camouflage in Clothing, 35
Canoes, 50, 54
Casting, 112-137
    Changing direction, 122, 124
    Distance and rod drift, 127
    Gauging the distance, 122, 125
    Letting out line, 122, 124
    Step-by-step sequence, 116, 117
Casting Plane, 118, 119, 122
Casting Stroke,
    Elements of, 116
Casts, types of,
    Distance, 126
    False, 122
    Overhead, 120
    Practicing, 115
    Reach, 133
    Roll, 130
Caterpillar, 67
CDC (Cul-de-Canard), 41
Chamois Leech, 71, 85
Chest Packs, 31
Chest Waders, 44-47
Chinook Salmon, 80
Chug Bug, 69
Cigar Grip, 12
Clinch Knot, 78, 98
Clothing, 30-35
Clouser Minnow, 73, 85, 92
Clouser's Crayfish, 71
Coho Salmon, 80
Color,
    Of clothing, 35
    Of flies, 56
    Of line, 22
Compound Leaders, 26
Corky Strike Indicator, 38
Cosseboom, 81
Crabs, Flies to Imitate, 73
Crappies,
    Equipment for, 83
    Flies for, 62, 64, 83
Crayfish,
    Crayfish flies for specific fish, 84, 86
    Flies to imitate, 60, 70, 71, 85
Crazy Charlie, 90
Creepy Cricket, 69, 82
Crickets, Flies to Imitate, 66, 69, 82
Crustaceans, 90
    Flies to imitate, 56, 60, 62, 63, 73
Cul-de-Canard, 41

D

Dahlberg Diving Bug, 87
Dahlberg's Mega Diver, 69, 72, 89
Dampening, 10, 11
Damselfly Nymph, 57
Dark Hendrickson Nymph, 61
Dave's Crayfish, 71, 85
Dave's Cricket, 66
Dave's Hopper, 79
Deep Water Squid, 73
Direct-Drive Reels, 16, 17
Direction of Cast, Changing,
    122, 124
Disc-Style Drag, 15
Distance Casting, 113, 126-129
    And rod drift, 126, 127
    Double haul, 126, 128
    Shooting line, 126
Distance, Gauging with False Cast,
    122, 125
Divers, 69
    For specific fish, 88, 89
    Specific patterns, 89
Double Haul, 126
    Step-by-step technique, 128, 129
Double-Line Connections, 108, 109
Double Surgeon's Knot, 100, 101
Double Surgeon's Loop, 102, 103
Double-Taper Line, 20
Downstream Mend, 132
    Step-by-step technique, 135
Down-Wing Dry Flies, 59
Drag,
    On dry fly, 132
    Disk-style, 15
    Ratchet-and-Pawl, 15
    See also: Palming, 16
Dropper Line, 38
Dry Flies, 82
    Diagram of elements, 58
    Floatants, 39
    Fly boxes for, 36, 37
    Leader length, 25
    Rods for, 10
    Specific patterns, 57-59
    Tying on, 78
    Used as strike indicator, 38
Drying a Waterlogged Fly, 39, 41, 122
Duncan Loop, 99

E

Egg Cluster, 71
Egg Flies, 70, 71, 80
Egg Sucking Leech, 79, 80
Elk-Hair Caddis, 82
Emerger Flies, 60, 61

F

False Casting, 113, 122
    Step-by-step technique, 123
    Various uses of the false cast,
        124, 125
Fanny Packs, 31
Fast-Action Fly Rods, 10
Feather-Wing Wet Flies, 63
Fiberglass Fly Rods, 9, 10, 112
Flats Boats, 50, 55
Flats Boots, 48
Floatants, 39
Floating Lines, 21
    Used as strike indicator, 38
    Weighting, 21
Floating/Sinking Lines, 22
Float Putty Strike Indicator, 38
Float Tubes, 50, 51, 53
Fluorocarbon Leaders,
    see: Polyvinelidene
Fly Boxes, 36, 37
Flying Ant, 77
Fly Lines, see: Line
Fly Size, and Tippet Diameter
    (chart), 27
Foam Adhesive Strike Indicator, 38
Forceps, 40, 78
Frogs,
    As fish food, 58
    Flies to imitate, 69, 85, 87, 88
Full-Wells Grip, 12
Fully-Dressed Salmon Flies, 63
Fur Ant, 66

G

Giant Black Stonefly Nymph, 61, 79
Gloves, 33
Gold Rat, 81
Goplin Emerger, 61
Gordon, 63
Gore-Tex® Wading Gear, 47
Graphite,
    Fly reels, 16
    Fly rods, 9, 10
Gravel Guards, 48
Greenheart Fly Rods, 8
Griffith's Gnat, 77
Grip Styles of Rods, 12
Gut Leaders, 25

H

Hackle-Wing Streamers, 65
Hair Popper, 69
Hair-Wing Wet Flies, 63
Half-Wells Grip, 12
Hand-Twist Retrieve, 136
    Step-by-step technique, 137
Hard-Bodied Slider, 69
Hats, 32
Heilgrammite, 79, 85
Hemingway Caddis, 59
Hemostat, 40
Henryville Special, 77
Hickory Fly Rods, 8
Hip Boots, 45
Homer Rhode Knot, 111
Hook Hone, 41
Hooks,
    Flattening barb, 40
    Removing, 40
    Sharpening, 41
    Sizes, 75
Hook Set, 10, 25
Hoppers, Flies to Imitate, 66, 79, 82
Horror, 90
Huff's Ballyhoo Tarpon Fly, 91
Hypothermia, Avoiding, 34

I

Imitator Flies,
    Defined, 56
    Selecting, 56, 57
Impressionistic Flies (defined), 56
Inchworm, 67
Insects,
    As fish food, 68, 76, 84
    Determining what trout are
        feeding on, 43
    Flies to imitate, 56, 58, 60, 62, 69
    See also: Terrestrials; specific insects

J

Jackets, Wading, 33
Jacklin's Hopper, 82
Janssen Black Marabou, 65
Jaw Spreaders, 89

K

Kick Boats and Fins, 50, 52, 53
Knotless Leaders, 26
Knots, 97-111
Knotted Leaders, 26
    Formulas for tying, 28, 29
Krystal Egg, 71

L

Landing Net, 42
Lani's Waller Waker, 81
Largemouth Bass, 84
    Equipment for, 86
    Flies for, 64, 86, 87
Leaders and Tippets, 25-29
    Adding weight, 37
    Adding wire leader to fly, 89
    Care, 27
    Diagram of parts, 26
    For various fish species, 77, 78,
        80-84, 86, 88, 90-93
    Knots to attach fly to tippet,
        98, 99
    Knots to attach shock tippet,
        108-110
    Knots to join line and leader,
        104, 105
    Knots to join sections, 100, 101, 107
    Knots to make loop in leader,
        102, 103
    Length, 26
    Material, 25
    Taper, 25, 26
    Tippet diameter, 26, 27
    Tool for straightening, 41
    Tying, 28, 29
    X-rating, 26, 27
Leader-Sink Compound, 78
Leader Straightener, 41
Lead-Eyed Egg Sucking Leech, 79
Leadwing Coachman, 82
Leeches, Flies to Imitate, 57, 71,
    79, 80, 85
Leech Flies, 71
    For specific fish, 84, 86
Lefty's Deceiver, 73, 89, 92, 93
Letting Out Line with False Cast,
    122, 124
Level Lines, 21
Light, 41
Light Spruce, 65, 79
Line, 18-24
    Backing, 23, 97
    Buoyancy, 21, 22
    Care, 22
    Color, 22
    Double-line connections, 108, 109
    Floating line used as strike
        indicator, 38
    For various fish species, 77, 78,
        80-84, 86, 88, 90-93
    How to get line out on water, 114
    How to string the rod, 114
    Knots for joining line and backing
        or leader, 104, 105
    Knot to make loop in line, 106
    Letting out with false cast, 122, 124
    Line weight chart, 19
    Mending line, 132-135

Nippers for cutting, 40
Parts of a fly line, 19
Retrieving, 136, 137
Taper, 20, 21
Weight, and rod length, 11
Llama, 79
Log Book, 43
Loop Knots, 102, 103, 106, 107, 111
Loop-to-Loop Connection, 106, 107

M

Magnifier, 41
Mandrel, 9, 10
Maps, 43
Marabou Streamers, 65
Martha's Vineyard Squid Fly, 73, 93
Matuka Streamer, 65
Mayflies, Flies to Imitate, 58, 59, 61
McCrab, 73
McKenzie Boats, 50, 55
Mending Line, 132-135
Messinger Frog, 87
Mice,
    As fish food, 68
    Flies to imitate, 69
Midges, Flies to imitate, 58
Mini-Pop, 82
Minnows, Flies to imitate, 62, 69, 85, 92
Modified Huffnagle Knot, 110
Modulus, 10, 112
MOE Bonefish, 90
Moldable Leader Weights, 37
Monofilament Leaders, 25
    Knots to join two sections, 100, 101
Mouserat, 69
Muddler Minnow, 65, 79, 83
Muddler Streamer Flies, 65
Multiplying Reel, 16
Muskies, see: Pike and Muskies

N

Neoprene Wading Gear, 45
Net, Landing, 42
Nippers, 40
No-Hackle Dry Flies, 59, 77
Northern Pike,
    Flies for, 64, 72
    Pike/muskie leader, formula for
        tying, 29
Nylon Leaders, 25
Nylon Wading Gear, 46
Nymphs,
    Diagram of elements, 60
    Fly boxes for, 37

For specific fish, 80, 82, 83
Rods for, 10
Specific patterns, 57, 60, 61
Strike indicators for, 38

O

Olive No-Hackle, 77
Olive Scud, 57, 61
Olive Thorax, 59
Olive Whit's Sculpin, 79
Overhand Knot, 97
Overhead Cast, 112, 113, 116
    Step-by-step technique, 120, 121

P

Pacific Salmon,
    Equipment for, 80
    Flies for, 80
Palmer-Hackle Wet Flies, 62, 63
Palming (defined), 16
Panfish, Flies for, 58, 60, 62, 66, 68,
    69, 71
Pan Pop, 82
Parachute Dry Flies, 59
Parmachene Belle, 57
Partridge-and-Yellow, 63
Peeking Caddis, 61
Perfection Loop, 103
Peterson's Giant Bunker, 93
Pheasant Tail Nymph, 57, 77, 82
Pike and Muskies,
    Equipment for, 88, 89
    Flies for, 64, 68, 72, 88, 89
    Pike/muskie leader, formula for
        tying, 29
Pink Salmon, 80
Pliers, 40
Polar Shrimp, 80
Polyvinelidene (PVDF) Leaders, 25
Popovic's Ultra Shrimp, 73, 90
Poppers, 69,
    For specific fish, 82, 88, 93
    Adding wire weedguard, 87
Prince Nymph, 77

R

Rafts, 50, 54
Rainbow Trout, 70, 77
    See also: Trout
Rain Gear, 32, 33

Ratchet-and-Pawl Drag, 15
Reach Cast, 133
Red Abbey, 63
Red Drum,
    see: Redfish
Redfish,
    Equipment for, 29, 92
    Flies for, 72, 73, 92
Red Quill, 59
Reels, 15-17
    Action, 16, 17
    Care, 17
    Diagram of parts, 15
    Drag, 15, 16
    Drive, 17
    Knot for attaching backing, 97
    Material, 16
    Size and capacity, 17
Reel Seats, 12
Renegade, 77
Retrieving Line, 136, 137
    Hand-twist retrieve, 137
    Strip retrieve, 136
Rod drift, 126, 127
Rods, 8-14
    Action, 10, 11
    Diagram of parts, 10, 11
    For various fish species, 77, 78,
       80-84, 86, 88, 90-93
    Grip style, 12
    How to string and hold, 114
    Length, 11
    Material, 8-10
    Reel seat, 12
    Rod type and casting distance,
       10, 112
    Weight, 11, 12
Roll-Casting, 113, 130
    And line taper, 20
    Step-by-step technique, 131
Royal Coachman,
    Bucktail streamer, 65
    Dry fly, 57
Rubber Wading Gear, 46
Running Line, 20
Rusty Rat, 81

S

Salmon,
    Equipment for, 80, 81
    Flies for, 58, 62, 64, 71, 80, 81
Salmon Eggs, 70
Salmon Flies, 63
    Fly boxes for, 37
Saltwater Fishing,
    Boats for, 55
    Clothing and gear for, 35, 48
    Equipment care, 17
    Flies, 64, 65, 72, 73

Formulas for tying leaders, 29
    Knots for, 108, 109
    Leaders for, 28, 29, 108
    Line for, 20
    Reels for, 16, 17
    Saltwater taper, 20
    Stripping basket for, 42
Sandals for Wading, 48
Scuds, Flies to Imitate, 57, 60, 61
Sculpin, Olive Whit's, 79
Searching Patterns (defined), 57
Seine, 43
Serendipity, 77
Shape of Flies, 57
Shock Tippet, 28, 88, 91
    Knots to attach to leader, 108-110
    Knot to attach to fly, 111
Shooting Head Line, see:
    Shooting Taper Line
Shooting Line Technique, 126
Shooting Taper Line, 20
Shrimp,
    As fish food, 72
    Flies to imitate, 60, 73, 80, 90, 92
Single-Action Reel, 16
Single Egg, 71, 80
Sinking Compound, 78
Sinking Lines, 21, 22, 88
    Leader length, 26
    Types, 21
Sink-Tip Lines, 22, 84
Size of Flies, 56
Skipping Bug, 73, 89, 93
Skunk, 80
Sliders, 69
Slow-Action Fly Rods, 10
Smallmouth Bass,
    Equipment for, 84
    Flies for, 64, 70, 71, 84, 85
Snails, 82
Snapping Shrimp, 90
Sneaky Pete, 85
Sockeye Salmon, 80
Soft-Hackle Wet Flies, 62, 63
Soles on Wading Gear, 47
Spawning Fish,
    Fishing techniques, 83
    Flies for, 68, 82, 83
Speed Stroke in Casting, 112, 116,
    117, 122
Spent-Wing Dry Flies, 59
Spey Rods, 81
Spiders, Flies to imitate, 59
Split-Cane, see: Bamboo Fly Rods
Split-Shot, 37
Sponge Bugs, 69, 82
Spotted Bass, Flies for, 64, 71
Squid Patterns, 73, 93
Steelhead,
    Equipment for, 15, 80
    Flies for, 71, 80
    Leader, formula for tying, 29

Stocking-Foot Waders, 44, 45
Stoneflies, Flies to Imitate, 58, 59,
    61, 79
Stop in Casting, 112, 116, 117
Streamers,
    Diagram of elements, 64
    Fly boxes for, 37
    For specific fish, 70, 80, 83, 84, 86,
       88, 91-93
    Specific patterns, 64, 65
Strike Indicators, 38
Striped Bass,
    Equipment for, 93
    Flies for, 64, 72, 73, 93
Stripping Basket, 21, 42
Stu Apte Black Death Plus, 91
Subsurface Flies, Leader Length, 25
Sunfish,
    Equipment for, 82
    Flies for, 62, 82

T

Tabory's Sand Lance, 93
Taper,
    Of leaders, 25, 26
    Of line, 20, 21
    Of rods, 10
Tarpon,
    Equipment for, 29, 91
    Flies for, 72, 91
Tarpon Cockroach, 91
Tarpon Orange/Yellow, 91
Teeny Steelhead Leech, 80
Terrestrial Flies, 82
    Diagram of elements, 66
    Specific patterns, 66, 67
Texture of Flies, 57
Thermometer, 40
Thorax Dry Flies, 59
Tippet, see: Leaders and Tippets
Toothy Fish, 89
    Flies for, 72
    Leaders for, 28, 29
Traditional Wet Flies, 63
Trico Spinner, 59
Trout,
    Equipment for, 76-78
    Flies for, 58, 60, 62, 64, 66, 70, 71,
       77-79
    Fly size vs. size of fish, 76
    See also specific species
Trout Leader, Formula for Tying, 28
Tube Knot, 105
Tubes, 50, 53
Tuna,
    Leader for, 29
Twist-On Strike Indicator, 38
Twist-On Weight, 37

U

Umpqua Swimming Baitfish, 89, 92
Undertaker, 63
Uni-Knot, 99
Upright-Wing Dry Flies, 59
Upstream Mend, 132
    Step-by-step technique, 134

V

Variant Dry Flies, 59
Vests, 30, 31

W

Wading Gear, 44-49
    Care, 49
    Materials, 46
    Sole types, 47
    Types, 44, 45
Wading Jackets, 33
Wading Technique, 49
Water Mend, 132, 134, 135
Water Skaters, Flies to Imitate, 59
Water Temperature, Measuring, 40
Weakfish, Flies for, 73

Weather and Clothing, 34
Weedguards, 64, 73, 88
    Adding to popper, 87
Weeds,
    Flies for fishing in, 64, 69, 86, 88
    Leaders for fishing in, 26
    Weedguards on flies, 64, 73, 87, 88
Weight Designations of Rods, 11
    And grip styles, 12
Weights of Fly Lines, 19
Weight-Forward Line, 20
Weights, 37
Wet Flies, 80, 82, 83
    Diagram of elements, 62
    Fly boxes for, 37
    Specific patterns, 57, 62, 63
Wet Wading, 45
Whistler, 89, 92
White Bass, Flies for, 64
White Miller, 83
Whitlock Salt Shrimp, 92
Whitlock's Hare Water Pup, 87
Whitlock's Hare Worm, 87
Whitlock's Near Nuff Frog, 85
Whit's Wiggle-Leg Frog, 69
Willow Fly Rods, 8
Wind,
    And casting, 116, 126
    And line selection, 20, 78
    And lure selection, 68, 69
    And rod selection, 75, 78
Wind Knots, 27
Wire Leader, 89
Wool Shad, 89

Wooly Bugger, 85
Wooly Worm, 63, 82

X

X-Rating, see: Leaders and Tippets

Y

Yarn Strike Indicator, 38
Yellow Sally, 83
Yellow Wooly Worm, 63

Z

Zinger, 40

Cy DeCosse Incorporated offers
a variety of how-to-books. For
information write:

    Cy DeCosse Subscriber Books
    5900 Green Oak Drive
    Minnetonka, MN 55343

Photo Credits

Note: **T**=Top, **C**=Center, **B**=Bottom, **L**=Left, **R**=Right, **I**=Inset

©**Billy Lindner,**
pp.4-5, p.31T, p.44T, p.70, p.72, p.88, p.91T.

©**Andy Anderson,**
p.32B, p.34T, p.80T.

©**Dale Spartas/The Green Agency,**
p.9C, p.33T, p.34B, p.55B, pp.94-95.

©**Victor H. Colvard/The Green Agency,**
p.54B, p.90T.

©**Charles Mohr/Photo Researchers,**
p.61BLI.

©**Tom Branch/Photo Researchers,**
p.61BRI.

©**Dale Spartas,**
p.81B.

©**David Sams,**
p.92T.